READING WOMEN

READING WOMEN

A Book Club Guide for Women's Fiction

Nanci Milone Hill

 LIBRARIES UNLIMITED

AN IMPRINT OF ABC-CLIO, LLC
Santa Barbara, California • Denver, Colorado • Oxford, England

Copyright 2012 by Nanci Milone Hill

Library of Congress Cataloging-in-Publication Data

Hill, Nanci Milone.
    Reading women : a book club guide for women's fiction / Nanci Milone Hill.
      pages cm
    Includes bibliographical references and index.
    ISBN 978–1–59158–802–3 (pbk.) — ISBN 978–1–59158–806–1 (ebook) 1. Women—Fiction—Bibliography. 2. American fiction—20th century—Bibliography. 3. American fiction—21st century—Bibliography. 4. American fiction—Women authors—Bibliography. 5. Chick lit—Bibliography. 6. American fiction—Women authors—Stories, plots, etc. 7. Women—Books and reading—United States. 8. Book clubs (Discussion groups)—United States. I. Title.
    Z1231.W85H45   2012
    [PS374.W6]
    016.813′6099287—dc23   2011043489

ISBN: 978–1–59158–802–3
EISBN: 978–1–59158–806–1

16 15 14 13 12   1 2 3 4 5

This book is also available on the World Wide Web as an eBook.
Visit www.abc-clio.com for details.

Libraries Unlimited
An Imprint of ABC-CLIO, LLC

ABC-CLIO, LLC
130 Cremona Drive, P.O. Box 1911
Santa Barbara, California 93116-1911

This book is printed on acid-free paper ∞

Manufactured in the United States of America

Contents

Acknowledgments

First and foremost, I would like to thank Neil Hollands and Barry Trott from the Williamsburg Regional Library for seeing something in me and passing along my name to Barbara Ittner at ABC-CLIO. Barry and Neil are two men I look up to for their wisdom and dedication to readers' services. I knew that if they believed in me, I could do this. Lucky for me, Barbara Ittner was looking for someone to write a guide book for women's fiction book groups and thought I had what it took to put together such a work. Barbara, you have been an amazing editor, not only putting up with my many missed deadlines but also shepherding me through the process of getting out a first book. Your insight and patience have been invaluable. I must also thank Arathi Pillai at PreMedia Global for her excellent editing skills. This book would not have been anywhere near ready for publication without her input.

Special thanks go to Bob Imhof, who not only believes in me, but has also been an excellent research assistant. No work on women's fiction would be complete without thanking the reading women in my own life. Thank you to my mother, Larraine Milone, my sisters, Silvia Milone Martin and Lori-ann Giamanco, and my daughter, Sarah Najat Al-Edwan. You are all intelligent, talented women in your own right, and my life is richer for having you in it. My grandmother, Sylvia Mitchell, told me at a very young age that I should be a writer. She would be so proud to see this book published. I love you Nana. Not a day goes by that I don't think of you and miss you. Leane Ellis, Readers' Advisory Librarian at the Lucius Beebe Memorial Library in Wakefield, Massachusetts, gave me my first taste of working with readers.[1] Leane holds in her head a vast amount of knowledge when it comes to readers' advisory services. She's my go-to gal for all things R.A., and I wouldn't be where I was today without her inspiration.

Introduction

Anyone who knows me knows that I'm head-over-heels in love with women's fiction, whether it be mainstream, romance or chick lit. In fact, I have often been known to start out my talks at conferences with the words "Hello, my name is Nanci Milone Hill and I am addicted to women's fiction." I am so addicted that I am always listening to one in the car during the day while I am reading one at home in the evening. Women's fiction touches me in a way no other fiction has. If a book is a journey, then women's fiction has allowed me to live many different lives. Through these novels I have been a Southern belle, a hip young CEO, a woman dealing with cancer or the loss of a loved one, and a woman besieged by friendship. Women's fiction speaks to me because it delves into the topics that are important in my own life—intimate relationships, friendship, overcoming loss—and it also offers hope for the future.

A self-proclaimed book group junkie as well, I guess it should have been no surprise when I found myself researching a book for women's fiction book groups.

The titles covered in this book represent only a very small portion of the books that I have either read or listened to over the years. For the purposes of brevity, I have limited my entries to novels published within the last 15 years, with the majority of them published in the last 10 years. Each entry includes an author biography, a brief summary of the book, bibliographic information, discussion questions, a link to the author's website when available, and a link to other online discussion guides for the title when available.

WHAT IS WOMEN'S FICTION?

Trying to find a definition of women's fiction is an exercise in futility. While several have tried to come up with a definition, nobody has quite been able to agree on one. Wikipedia describes it as "an umbrella term for a wide-ranging collection of literary sub-genres that are marketed to female readers, including many mainstream novels, romantic fiction, 'chick lit' and other sub-genres . . . Although sometimes used synonymously, it is distinguished from Women's writing which deals with literature written by (rather than targeted at) women."[1] On June 4, 2009, blogger Barbara Vey asked the question "What Is Women's Fiction?" Some responders said that women's fiction was "anything that women write that appeals to women." A man who responded said it was "anything they want to read for escapism." A female respondent said it was "anything that touches your soul and makes you feel better about life."[2] Are you beginning to see why women's fiction is so hard to define? From a publisher's standpoint, it *is* about whom these books are marketed to. Because that is the case, mainstream fiction, romance, and chick lit get thrown into the same generic melting pot. However, as Kristie Camacho points out in her article "What Is Women's Fiction?"[3] romance, chick lit, and women's fiction aren't the same thing anymore than horror, suspense, and mystery are the same genre.

According to the Romance Writers of America, a romance novel must contain two basic elements. First of all, it must feature a central love story. While there may be several subplots in the novel, the main story deals with two people falling in love. Secondly, to qualify as a romance novel, a book must have an emotionally satisfying ending.[4] The romance genre is broken down into many subgenres, including Christian romance (in which the presence of God in the characters' lives helps them find happiness), historical romance (taking place at least 50 years before the date of publication), and paranormal romance (in which one of the main love interests is a vampire, werewolf, angel, or other paranormal creature), not to mention many, many others.

How does romance differ from chick lit? According to professor Suzanne Ferris, chick lit is a genre of fiction that is humorous and lighthearted. It features female protagonists in their 20s and early 30s who are single and career-driven.[5] *Library Journal* refutes that definition. Rebecca Vnuk, author of *Read On . . . Women's Fiction: Reading Lists for Every Taste* and *Women's Fiction Authors: A Research Guide*, agrees that while the tone of chick lit is usually more humorous and lighthearted, it does not always necessarily feature young, single women. She notes the recent popularity of mommy lit, which features married women who either want to become pregnant or have recently had children. She argues that chick lit "almost always posits young women setting out to make their mark on the world."[6] Like romance, chick lit is broken down into several subgenres. Vnuk lists them as Brit lit or "singletons" (think *Bridget Jones's Diary*), lad lit (chick lit for men), workplace tell all, ethnic chick lit, bride lit, mommy lit, widow lit, Christian chick lit, mystery chick lit, and hen lit (aimed at 40- to 60-year-olds).

While the term *women's fiction* has become an umbrella term of sorts that includes both romance and chick lit, for the purpose of this work, we will look at mainstream women's fiction as a separate entity. My definition of mainstream women's fiction is fiction that is almost always written by, for, and about women. It deals with the issues that are important in women's lives: family, marriage, divorce, aging, friendship, infidelity, and overcoming obstacles to happiness and fulfillment. The characters in these novels may be any age. Some titles, such as *The Girls' Guide to Hunting and Fishing* by Melissa Bank, follow the protagonist from a young age through adulthood. Others, such as Ann B. Ross' *Miss Julia* series, feature an older main character. Still others deal with women facing middle age. No matter what the age of the main character, she is bound to be facing some issue, the resolution of which will make her a stronger person.

I want to make note of the fact that while my definition includes the words *almost always for, by and about women*, there are certain men who write women's fiction and do it well. I will always remember finishing *Midwives* by Chris Bohjalian and turning the last page to discover that the author was a male! The many throngs of Nicholas Sparks fans attest to the fact that there's something about the stories he tells that reaches his female audience. I would argue, however, that men who get women's fiction *right* are the exception to the rule. By and large, you will find books marketed to women that succeed are written by women. Argue with me all you want, that's my definition, and I'm sticking to it.

Okay, so obviously women's fiction is popular, but how discussable is it? Many book groups poo-poo the idea of discussing women's fiction, dismissing it as fluff without enough meat for discussion. Those groups don't know what they are missing out on. For starters, many book groups are already discussing women's fiction and just don't know it. How many book groups have discussed *Belong to Me* by Marisa de los Santos or *Lucia, Lucia* by Adriana Trigiani? How many readers have discussed Ruth's path to understand her aging mother in Amy Tan's *The Bonesetter's Daughter*? Why do libraries still, in May of 2011, have such a wait list for Susan Elizabeth Phillips's *Call Me Irresistible*? It's because these titles touch on subjects and themes that are important to women, and who would ever argue that women can't talk about issues with each other?

GENERAL BOOK DISCUSSION PROCEDURES

Whether you are a member of an existing book group, you are looking to joining a book group, or you want to start one yourself, these are some good rules to follow if you want to ensure a productive discussion in which everyone who wants to talk has a chance to.

1. Make sure everyone introduces herself. Sometimes you will have new members join, and it's good for everyone to feel welcome. I always have everyone answer the question "Did you like the book?" as an icebreaker.
2. It's okay to disagree. Some of the best book group discussions I've participated in are ones in which people had different ideas about the theme of the book, the likeability of a character, or the way the novel ended.
3. It's okay to hate the book. The best meeting I remember was a discussion of Ron Hansen's novel *Hitler's Niece*. Sometimes discussing why you hated a book is just as productive as discussing why you loved it.
4. Everyone who wants to talk should have a chance to. We have all been part of book groups in which one person hogs the floor. A good discussion leader will make sure everyone has a chance to speak. To head off discussion hogs, I usually go around the table before getting into the meat of the discussion so that everyone has a chance to comment. Those who don't wish to talk can simply pass. Those who might be too timid to speak up but would really like to contribute get a chance to.
5. Try to stay on topic. Personal stories can add a great deal to the discussion when they stick to the topic at hand, but it's very easy for someone to get caught up in telling a personal story that doesn't really relate to the book. If you're the discussion leader, it's your job to nip that in the bud.
6. No interrupting people while they speak. Oftentimes this happens because someone is enthusiastic about what another person has to say and wants to agree with her. As the group leader, you can say something like "hold that thought."

SAMPLE DISCUSSION QUESTIONS FOR BOOK GROUPS

This general list of book discussion questions should help you get a discussion started for any work of fiction. Questions specific to each title are included with each entry.

1. Did you enjoy the book? Why or why not?
2. What themes were present throughout the novel?
3. Who was your favorite character in the novel and why?
4. Was the setting important to the story? Could the novel have been set somewhere else and still have been as successful?

5. Was the time period important to the novel? Could the novel have taken place during another time period and been just as effective? Why or why not?
6. Was the narrator a reliable one?
7. Have you read other books by this author? How does this book compare to the author's other novels?
8. Would you recommend this book to others? Who would you recommend it to and why?

Chapter 1
Ninety Titles for Discussion

Elizabeth Adler

The House in Amalfi

Elizabeth Adler was born in 1950 in Yorkshire, England. She met her husband (an American) while working in London. The two have lived many places, including Brazil, France, England, Ireland, and the United States. The couple has one daughter, Belle, who graduated from Harvard and now works as an architect.

Adler published her first book, *Léonie*, in 1985. It was simultaneously published in the U.K. under the title *Private Desire*. Since that time, Adler has published 20 novels. Her works have been translated into 22 languages. She writes both mystery and romance novels, often combining the two genres. Adler has also published under the name Ariana Scott.

Plot Summary: Lamour Harrington has spent the two years following her husband's death in a state of mourning. Her work as a landscape architect keeps her busy but has not been enough to withdraw her from her solitude. When she learns through a friend that her husband was planning on leaving her the night he died, she decides to travel to the Amalfi Coast, to the place she lived as a young girl with her reclusive father, Jon-Boy. While there, she meets two charming men and unearths the secret of her father's death.

Publication Date: 2005

Number of Pages: 368

Geographic Setting: Chicago, Rome, and Amalfi

Time Period: Present day

Series Notes: This is a stand-alone novel.

Subject Headings: Amalfi (Italy), Americans in Italy. Family secrets. Fiction—Depression in women Domestic fiction

Appeal Points: Descriptive settings and fully developed characters are Adler's trademark. This novel features both, plus a romantically satisfying story laced with mystery.

DISCUSSION QUESTIONS

- Jammy decides to tell Lamour what she knows about the night her husband died. Do you think this was a good idea? What would you do in a similar situation?
- Discuss Lamour's relationship with Mifune. What role does he play in helping her find herself?
- Lamour is attracted to both Lorenzo and Nico. Were you satisfied with who she ends up with? Why or why not?
- Do you believe that you can ever recapture the happiness of childhood?
- Several secrets are revealed throughout the course of the novel. Is it ever good to keep secrets? Does finding the answers she's looking for help Lamour to know her father better?
- The setting is a character in and of itself in this novel. Where in the book do we see this?

WEBSITE

http://www.elizabethadler.net

READERS' GUIDE

None available.

READ-ALIKES

Edwards-Jones, Imogene. *Tuscany for Beginners*—for similar setting, pacing and similar storyline.

Mayle, Peter. *A Good* Year—for rich scenic descriptions.

Roberts, Nora. *Jewels of the Sun*—for similar themes and writing style.

Sarah Addison Allen

Garden Spells

Sarah Addison Allen was born in Asheville, North Carolina, the daughter of an award-winning newspaper columnist and a housewife mother. She has one sister, Sydney. Allen received her B.A. in literature.

Plot Summary: The Waverly women have always been different. Claire is a caterer who uses cooking to reach a desired end. Her sister Sydney followed in their mother's footsteps, moving far away in an attempt to escape her own destiny. Sydney's daughter Bay knows where things belong. Their cousin Evanelle gives people gifts that they don't yet know they will need. When Sydney and Bay flee from their abusive home, they return to Bascom, North Carolina. Sydney reverts to her maiden name, Bay assumes a new identity and enrolls in school, and the sisters try to get along. Add a fruit-throwing tree, a handsome neighbor, and an old high school rivalry, and you have the makings of a fantastic tale that builds until its explosive finale.

Publication Date: 2007

Number of Pages: 320

Geographic Setting: Bascom, North Carolina

Time Period: Present day

Series Notes: This is a stand-alone novel.

Subject Headings: Sisters—Fiction; North Carolina—Fiction; Domestic Fiction; Magic realist fiction; Gardening—Fiction

Appeal Points: Readers of Southern fiction will revel in the small-town setting and interpersonal relationships as they are developed throughout the story. A leisurely pace infused with sporadic humor makes this an engaging tale.

DISCUSSION QUESTIONS

- Discuss the biblical symbolism of the apple tree as it is presented in the novel.

- Sydney and Claire both suffer from abandonment issues. How has each of these characters handled abandonment? Who have they been abandoned by?
- Sydney's magic revolves around the cutting of hair. Claire has a gift with food. If you could have one magical power, what would it be, and why?
- Small-town stereotypes abound in the novel. What characters reflect these stereotypes?
- Both sisters are running from something or someone in the novel. Who and what are they running from?
- Do you think Emma's behavior toward Sydney is typical of a Southern debutante? Do you think she would have behaved differently if the story had been set in another location?
- Given Emma's manipulative character, why do you think Hunter John loves her?
- What do you believe Sydney's life would have been like if she had stayed in Bascom when she was younger? Do you think the relationship with Hunter John would have worked? Would Sydney and Claire have been closer?
- If you could do something to reveal your future, would you do it?
- Do you believe in fate?
- Would you consider this a Southern novel? Why or why not?

WEBSITE

http://www.sarahaddisonallen.com

READERS' GUIDE

http://www.barnesandnoble.com/bookstore/recommended.asp?PID=19070
http://www.readinggroupguides.com/guides_G/garden_spells1.asp

READ-ALIKES

Barry, Brunonia. *The Lace Reader*—for magical realism and similar themes.
Esquivel, Laura. *Like Water for Chocolate*—for magical realism and quirky characters.
Hoffman, Alice. *Practical Magic*—for magical realism and similar themes.

Susan Andersen

Bending the Rules

Susan Andersen grew up in Seattle, Washington, the only girl among three children. She trained as a dental assistant but did not enjoy the work. Her first book, *Shadow Dance*, was published in 1989. Susan has been named a Career Achievement Award Winner by *Romantic Times* magazine. She married her high school sweetheart and had one son. The couple currently resides in Washington State.

Plot Summary: Seattle artist Poppy Calloway is a free spirit. As far as Detective Jason de Sanges is concerned, she's a major pain in the behind, especially when three teenagers are arrested for marking downtown storefronts with graffiti and Poppy suggests they paint a mural for their community service hours. Jason is ordered to oversee the project by his supervisor, who thinks it will bring the department good press. Poppy and Jason are about as different as can be, but that does not stop the sparks from flying in this feel-good romp.

Publication Date: 2009

Number of Pages: 379

Geographic Setting: Seattle, Washington

Time Period: Present day

Series Notes: This is the second book in the *Sisterhood Diaries* series.

Subject Headings: Contemporary romances, Seattle (WA)—Fiction; Pacific Northwest literature

Appeal Points: Fast pace, sexual tension, humor, and well-developed characters.

DISCUSSION QUESTIONS

- Jason and Poppy were brought up in very different circumstances. Poppy was raised on a commune; Jason grew up in foster care. How do you think their childhoods impacted on the adults they became?

- Though Jason and Poppy come from different backgrounds, they find common ground. In what ways are they similar?
- Why do you think Jason is such a stickler for the rules?
- Describe the relationship between Poppy and her friends.
- Describe Poppy's relationship with the teens. Describe Jason's relationship with the teens. Do these relationships change over time? How?
- Do you believe that community service is a deterrent to vandalism?

WEBSITE

http://www.susanandersen.com/

READERS' GUIDE

None available.

READ-ALIKES

Kelley, Karen. *Temperature's Rising*—for similar pacing and tone.
Linz, Cathy. *Bad Girls Don't*—for similar pacing and tone.
Sneed, Tamara. *You've Got a Hold on Me*—for sexual tension, pacing, and similar subject.

Mary Kay Andrews

Deep Dish

Mary Kay Andrews is the pseudonym for Kathy Hogan Trocheck. Andrews was born in 1954 in St. Petersburg, Florida. She earned a bachelor's degree in journalism from the University of Georgia. After graduation, she worked as a journalist for several newspapers. While in Savannah, Georgia, she was assigned to cover a murder trial, on which the novel *Midnight in the Garden of Good and Evil* by John Berendt was based. In 1991, she left journalism to pursue a career as a novelist. Her first novel, titled *Every Crooked Nanny*, was published in 1992 and introduced the Callahan family. She has written two mystery series under her own name. Several of her mystery titles have been nominated for the Edgar, Anthony, Agatha, and Macavity Awards. She also publishes Southern women's fiction under the name Mary Kay Andrews. She and her husband Tom currently reside in Atlanta, Georgia. They have two grown children.

Plot Summary: Gina Foxton hosts her own cooking show on local cable television. When her show gets canceled and she finds out that her producer boyfriend has been cheating on her, she decides to go for the gold and become the next big name on the Cooking Chanel. The only thing standing in her way is Tate Moody, a.k.a. "Mr. Kill It and Grill It." Tate is all man, which in Gina's estimation is so *not* a good thing. The producers of the Cooking Chanel see dollar signs, however, and pit the two against each other on a television cook-off. Soon fish is not the only thing flying.

Publication Date: 2008

Number of Pages: 400

Geographic Setting: Atlanta, Georgia

Time Period: Present day

Series Notes: This is a stand-alone novel.

Subject Headings: Women cooks—Fiction; Television—Fiction; Atlanta (GA)—Fiction; Love stories—American

Appeal Points: A quick, humorous read with delightful characters.

DISCUSSION QUESTIONS

- There are recipes throughout the novel. Which one would you like to try?
- What role does Tate's dog, Moonpie, play in getting Gina and Tate together?
- What role does location play in Tate and Gina's romance?
- Why is Gina reluctant to get involved with Tate?
- Describe Gina's relationship with her sister.
- Discuss Gina and Lisa's relationship with each other.
- Discuss Gina and Lisa's relationship with their mother.
- Why do you think men cheat?

WEBSITE

http://marykayandrews.com/blog/index.asp?id=home

READERS' GUIDE

http://www.harpercollins.com/author/authorExtra.aspx?authorID=20217
&isbn13=9780060837365&displayType=readingGuide

READ-ALIKES

Crusie, Jennifer. *Agnes and the Hitman*—for similar tone and style.
Evanovich, Janet. *Love Overboard*—for similar themes and tone.
Ray, Jeanne. *Eat Cake*—for similar subject matter and tone.

Donna Ball

A Year on Ladybug Farm

Donna Ball was born in northern Georgia in 1951. She published her first book in 1982. She also writes under the pseudonyms Rebecca Flanders, Donna Carlisle, Leigh Bristol, Taylor Brady, and Donna Boyd. Together, she has more than 80 works of commercial fiction to her credit. In addition to her writing, she runs an online dog training company called The Pet Coach. Donna and her four dogs live in a restored nineteenth-century barn in the heart of the Blue Ridge Divide.

Plot Summary: Three middle-aged friends, Lindsey, Bridget, and Cici, find themselves alone now that the children are grown and the husbands are gone. They decide to pool their funds to purchase and refurbish a run-down mansion. At Ladybug Farm, the women feel sure that they will each be able to reinvent their lives. Over the course of a year, they grapple with bug infestations, wayward sheep, a ghostly roommate, and a garden thief, all the while learning that they are not too old to change their lives.

Publication Date: 2009

Number of Pages: 374

Geographic Setting: Shenandoah River Valley, Virginia

Time Period: Present day

Series Notes: This is the first book in a two-book series.

Subject Headings: Female friendship—Fiction; Dwellings—Maintenance and repair—Fiction; Shenandoah River Valley (Virginia and West Virginia)—Fiction

Appeal Points: Strong sense of place and attention to detail.

DISCUSSION QUESTIONS

- Each of the three main characters leaves behind her old life to live on Ladybug Farm. What is each woman leaving behind? What is each one searching for?

- How well does each of the women deal with the complications that arise over the course of the year?
- Did you feel it was realistic for the women to drop everything and purchase the mansion?
- Ball does an excellent job of describing place. What are some sections where she does this especially well?
- Have you ever regretted your choices? Wanted to start life over? What did you do to overcome the need for change?

WEBSITE

http://www.donnaball.net/

READERS' GUIDE

None available.

READ-ALIKES

Buchan, Elizabeth. *The Good Wife Strikes Back*—for similar theme and humor.

Pemberton, Margaret. *The Four of Us*—for similar themes and attention to descriptions.

Radish, Kris. *Dancing Naked at the Edge of Dawn*—for similar themes.

Heather Barbieri

The Lace Makers of Glenmara: A Novel

Heather Barbieri majored in English at the University of Washington. Before turning her hand to fiction, she worked on the editorial staff of several magazines and papers, eventually writing feature articles. Her first novel, *Snow in July*, was published by Soho Press in 2004. That publication won her applause as a Book Sense Pick and a *Library Journal* Notable Book. *The Lace Makers of Glenmara* is her second novel. She is currently at work on a third. Barbieri resides in Seattle with her husband and three children.

Plot Summary: In the wake of her breakup with long-time boyfriend Ethan and the death of her mother, Kate Robinson flees to the small Irish town of Glenmara, where she hopes to get in touch with her roots and heal from her losses. While in Glenmara, she is taken under the wings of several members of the local lace-making group. The women she meets, Bernie, Oona, Colleen, and Aileen, each share their stories with her, little by little letting her into their circle. A plot to use the women's lace to create a new line of magical lingerie and a taste of romance for Kate add to the plotline.

Publication Date: 2009

Number of Pages: 288

Geographic Setting: Seattle; Glenmara, Ireland

Time Period: Present day

Series Notes: This is a stand-alone novel.

Subject Headings: Fashion designers—Fiction; Americans—Ireland—Fiction; Female Friendship—Fiction

Appeal Points: A quaint story featuring female friendships, some controversy, and a light romance.

DISCUSSION QUESTIONS

- What role does lace making play in the story?
- What relationships change over the course of the novel? How do they change?

- The story takes place in a small town. How would the story be different if it were set in a large city?
- Discuss the idea of religion in the novel.
- Discuss the character of Father Byrne. Is he truly a villain? Does he have any redeeming qualities?
- What do you think happens to Kate and Sullivan after the last page?

WEBSITE

http://www.heatherbarbieri.com/

READERS' GUIDE

http://www.heatherbarbieri.com/

READ-ALIKES

Binchy, Maeve. *Heart and Soul*—for similar theme of a community caught between the old and the new. Similar setting.

Jacobs, Kate. *The Friday Night Knitting Club*—for similar themes.

Kelly, Cathy. *Just Between Us*—for similar themes and setting.

Lois Battle

The Floramamba Ladies' Auxiliary and Sewing Circle

Lois Battle was born in 1940 in Subiaco, Western Australia. She moved to the United States in 1946 following the death of her father and her mother's remarriage to a man in the U.S. Navy. Battle is the author of seven novels. She currently resides in Beaufort, South Carolina.

Plot Summary: Five women come together, become friends, and learn that life can change in a moment. Bonnie Cullman's world is turned upside down when her husband announces that he has lost their vast fortune and that he is leaving her. Suddenly finding herself without a roof over her head or a dime to her name, she takes a job teaching a course at a community college. The job requires her to move from Atlanta to Floramamba, Alabama. It is there that she meets Hilly, Celia, Albertine, and Ruth. The women enroll in a course for displaced homemakers when the lingerie factory that employed them closes. Though the other four women are used to dealing with less, it is a hard lesson for Bonnie to learn. Through laughter and friendship, all five women find happiness and satisfaction.

Publication Date: 2001

Number of Pages: 358

Geographic Setting: Floramamba, Alabama

Time Period: Present day

Series Notes: This is a stand-alone novel.

Subject Headings: Women—Friendship—Alabama; Middle-aged women—Alabama; Small-town life—Alabama

Appeal Points: Battle writes believable flawed but likeable characters. She has a keen eye for setting with an attention to detail.

DISCUSSION QUESTIONS

- Bonnie goes from having it all to having nothing. How does this change affect her confidence in herself over the course of the novel?

- How does losing their jobs affect Hilly, Celia, Albertine, and Ruth?
- The saying goes that when a door closes, somewhere a window opens. Is that true for the women in this novel?
- Discuss how money, having it or not having it, shapes our outlook in life.
- Have you ever suffered a terrible blow? Did you learn something from it?
- Do you think the novel is uniquely Southern? Could these characters and these situations happen anywhere else? If so, how do you think the characters' reactions might have differed?
- Describe Bonnie's relationship with Riz. How is it different from her relationship with Devoe? Where do you think their relationship will lead them?
- Discuss the men in the novel. How are they similar? Different?

WEBSITE

The author does not have a website.

READERS' GUIDE

http://us.penguingroup.com/static/rguides/us/florabama_ladies_auxiliary.html
http://www.readinggroupguides.com/guides3/florabama_ladies_auxiliary1.asp

READ-ALIKES

Gillespie, Karin. *A Dollar Short: A Bottom Dollar Girls Novel*—for similar setting and themes.
Kelly, Cathy. *Best Friends: A Novel*—for similar themes.
Wells, Rebecca. *Ya-Yas in Bloom*—for similar setting and themes.

Elizabeth Berg

The Year of Pleasures

Elizabeth Berg was born on December 2, 1948, in St. Paul, Minnesota. At the age of three, her father re-enlisted in the army. She spent her growing years moving from one place to another. She worked as a registered nurse for 10 years before turning her hand to writing. She was married for 20 years before divorcing and has two children as a result of that marriage. She now lives with her partner, Bill, and their dog outside of Chicago. They also have a home in Wisconsin.

Plot Summary: Following the death of her husband, Bostonian Betta Nolan follows through on their dream to move to a small town in the Midwest and live life simply. Her journey takes her to Stewart, Illinois, where she buys an old Victorian house. There she makes friends with her handsome handyman Tom, her 10-year-old neighbor, and a hardened old man. She also reaches out to her three college friends whom she has not seen in years.

Publication Date: 2005

Number of Pages: 224

Geographic Setting: Stewart, Illinois

Time Period: Present day

Series Notes: This is a stand-alone novel.

Subject Headings: Women—Friendship; Grief—Fiction; Small-town life—Illinois; Love stories, American

Appeal Points: Those looking for an emotional ride will enjoy Betta's journey from grief to self-fulfillment. Berg does an excellent job of describing small-town life.

DISCUSSION QUESTIONS

- We are led to understand that Betta was very happy and secure in her life with John. Over the course of the novel, she finds joy once again. Do you believe she could have achieved such fulfillment and self-awareness if she had not lost John?

- Betta believes that we become even closer to our loved ones after their death. Do you believe this to be true? Discuss how this plays out in the novel. Have you ever had such an experience?

- Do you believe that happiness lies in the simple things in life? What simple things bring you pleasure?

- Food plays an important part in the novel. How so? It is often said that the kitchen is the most used part of any home. Do you believe this to be true? Why do you think the kitchen is an important place?

- Following her marriage to John, Betta lost touch with her friends from college, yet when she calls them, they come running to her side. Do you believe that true friends can pick up right where they left off, no matter how much time has passed? Have you had this experience in your life?

WEBSITE

http://www.elizabeth-berg.net/

READERS' GUIDE

http://www.bookbrowse.com/reading_guides/detail/index.cfm?book_number =1564

READ-ALIKES

Hood, Anne. *Somewhere Off the Coast of Maine*—for women's friendships and themes of overcoming obstacles.

King, Cassandra. *The Same Sweet Girls*—for similar lyrical style and themes.

Quindlen, Anna. *Blessings: A Novel*—for similar lyrical style.

Susan Breen

The Fiction Class

Susan Breen was born Susan Zelony on October 4, 1956, in Forest Hills, New York. Breen received her B.A. in political science from the University of Rochester. She received her M.A. in international affairs at Columbia University, where she specialized in Russian economics. Before turning her hand to fiction, she worked as a reporter. Her first job was writing for *Fortune Magazine*. Breen and her husband of 25 years currently reside in Manhattan, where she teaches Beginning Fiction and Advanced Fiction at the Gotham Writer's Workshop. They have four children.

Plot Summary: Arabella Hicks is a 38-year-old copy editor and fiction writing teacher. When she's not writing or teaching, she's visiting her mother Vera in a nursing home, where she suffers from Parkinson's disease.

Arabella has spent the last seven years rewriting her novel, not able to find an ending that will satisfy her. Nor is she satisfied with her relationship with her mother or her own nonexistent love life.

Publication Date: 2008

Number of Pages: 336

Geographic Setting: Manhattan, New York City

Time Period: Present day

Series Notes: This is a stand-alone novel.

Subject Headings: Mothers and daughters—Fiction; Women teachers—Fiction; Parent and adult child—Fiction; Nursing homes—Fiction

Appeal Points: A quick-moving novel with in-depth characters who overcome obstacles.

DISCUSSION QUESTIONS

- What themes are presented throughout the novel?
- What did you think of Arabella? Did the way you felt about her change over the course of the novel? If so, what brought about that change?

- Discuss Arabella's relationship with Vera. What events in their past made it so stunted?
- Vera's story acts as a catalyst for the change between her and her daughter. Why?
- Do you believe that fiction imitates reality? Do Arabella and Vera's stories tell us anything about their reality?
- Chuck and Arabella become involved. Do you think he is a good choice for Arabella? Why or why not? Do you believe they will stay together?
- Did you like the ending of the novel? Why or why not?

WEBSITE

http://www.thefictionclass.com/

READERS' GUIDE

http://us.penguingroup.com/static/rguides/us/fiction_class.html

READ-ALIKES

Delinsky, Barbara. *Shades of Grace*—for similar themes.
Levine, Michael. *Not Me: A Novel*—for similar themes.
Miller, Sue. *The Distinguished Guest*—for similar themes and style.

Elizabeth Buchan

Revenge of the Middle-Aged Woman

Elizabeth Buchan worked as a blurb writer for Penguin Books and as a fiction editor at Random House before turning her hand to writing. She has published a biography of Beatrix Potter for children as well as six adult novels. She lives in London with her husband and two children.

Plot Summary: A middle-aged book editor for a London newspaper loses her husband of 25 years and her job in the same day. Criticized by her mother and blamed for the failure of her marriage, Rose takes solace in the bottle. Then her beloved cat dies, her daughter Poppy gets married without her, and her mother falls ill. Rose decides enough is enough. While taking the bull by the horns, she fondly remembers an old love and an exquisite visit to Rome during her youth. Rose eventually proves that revenge is indeed sweet.

Publication Date: 2003

Number of Pages: 352

Geographic Setting: London

Time Period: Present day

Series Notes: The story is continued in a sequel, *Wives Behaving Badly*.

Subject Headings: Middle-aged women—Fiction; Life change events—Fiction; Married women—Fiction; Adultery—Fiction; England—Fiction

Appeal Points: Buchan, best known for her romance novels, here draws insightful, believable characters who struggle on their journey to self-discovery. A satisfying ending and intermittent humor will appeal to readers.

DISCUSSION QUESTIONS

- Rose loved Hal, but he wanted to travel. Do you think she made the right decision leaving Hal and marrying Nathan?
- Describe Rose's relationship with her children.

- Were there warning signs in Rose's marriage that she failed to see?
- Do you think Poppy's marriage will last?
- Describe Rose's relationship with her mother.
- How would the book have been different if told from a man's perspective?
- Friends are a comfort for us during times of need. Do you remember times when your friends were a comfort to you?

WEBSITE

http://www.elizabethbuchan.com/

READERS' GUIDE

http://www.readinggroupguides.com/guides3/revenge_of_the_middle-aged
   _woman1.asp

READ-ALIKES

Berg, Elizabeth. *The Year of Pleasures*—for similar themes and style.
Kelman, Judith. *Backward in High Heels*—for similar themes.
Radish, Kris. *Dancing Naked at the Edge of Dawn*—for similar themes and tone.

Paula Morantz Cohen

Jane Austen in Boca

Paula Morantz Cohen holds the position of Distinguished Professor of English at Drexell University. She has written and published two nonfiction novels. *Jane Austen in Boca* is her first work of fiction. Cohen and her husband reside in Moorestown, New Jersey.

Plot Summary: In this contemporary rewrite of Jane Austen's *Pride and Prejudice*, three Jewish widows become friends at a retirement community in Boca Raton, Florida. May Newman is perfectly content with her life until her daughter-in-law Carol decides to play matchmaker. Perpetual redhead Lila Katz is on the lookout for husband number two. Retired academic librarian Flo Kilman is their ever-acerbic sidekick, who is none too pleased with May's sweetheart's best friend Stan. Full of satire, Cohen's debut novel is sure to win the hearts of snowbirds and younger folk alike.

Publication Date: 2002

Number of Pages: 288

Geographic Setting: Boca Raton, Florida

Time Period: Present day

Series Notes: This is a stand-alone novel

Subject Headings: Courtship—Fiction; Families—Fiction; Boca Raton (Florida)—Fiction

Appeal Points: Humorous novel with well-drawn characters. Wonderful social commentary.

DISCUSSION QUESTIONS

- The novel is based on Jane Austen's *Pride and Prejudice*. Compare Cohen's characters with their Austen counterparts.
- How does the plot differ from Austen's novel?

- Describe the friendship among May, Lila, and Flo. Would their friend-ship look any different if they were younger women?
- The novel is set in a community for retired Jewish folk. Do you think the novel would be different if not for the ethnic variable? How so?
- How do you think the novel would differ if the residents were Italian or Spanish instead of Jewish?
- Cohen does an excellent job of social commentary. Discuss scenes from the novel in which this is particularly evident.
- Mothers-in-law often get a bad rap for being interfering. In Cohen's novel, it is the daughter-in-law, Carol, who is interfering. Discuss the relationship between the two women.

WEBSITE

The author does not have a website.

READERS' GUIDE

http://www.readinggroupguides.com/guides3/jane_austen_in_boca1.asp

READ-ALIKES

Ledbetter, Suzann. *Half Way to Half Way*—for similar themes and tone.
Ross, Ann B. *Miss Julia Hits the Road*—for similar tone.
Sawyer, Corrine Holt. *The J. Alfred Prufrock Murders*—for similar themes and tone.

Claire Cook

The Wildwater Walking Club

Cook was born in Alexandria, Virginia, in 1955. She majored in film and creative writing at Syracuse University. Before turning her hand to fiction, Cook worked as an aerobics instructor, advertising copywriter, and creative writing instructor. Her first novel, *Ready to Fall*, was published in 2000. Her second novel, *Must Love Dogs*, was published in 2002 and then made into a feature film starring Diane Lane and John Cusack. Cook and her husband have two grown children. They live in Scituate, Massachusetts.

Plot Summary: Noreen Kelly has identified herself by her work for the last 18 years. When she accepts a buyout from her job, she is hopeful about all the time she will have to do the things she's longed to do. What she finds is plenty of time to contemplate the mistakes she's made in her life. With a new determination, she puts on a pair of sneakers and starts walking. Soon she is joined by her next-door neighbor Tess, who thought she'd be spending breezy days with her college-bound daughter until her daughter stops speaking to her. Finally, they are joined by Rosie, who moved her family back to her parents' lavender farm following her mother's death. As they women walk and talk, friendships are formed and problems are solved.

Publication Date: 2009

Number of Pages: 256

Geographic Setting: Coastal Massachusetts

Time Period: Present day

Series Notes: This is a stand-alone novel

Subject Headings: Neighbors—Fiction; Middle-aged women—Fiction; Female friendship—Fiction

Appeal Points: Quick pacing, believable dialogue. Lighthearted and humorous tone.

DISCUSSION QUESTIONS

- Who do you most relate to—Noreen, Tess, or Rosie? Why?
- How does each of the main characters change over the course of the novel? What instigates that change?
- Discuss the character of Michael. Does he have any redeeming qualities? Have you ever allowed a man to sway you into making a major decision?
- Discuss Tess's relationship with her daughter.
- Do you believe Rosie did the right thing moving her family home? Would you have made such a sacrifice? Why or why not?
- The women in the novel are brought together through walking. What activities have brought you together with your friends?

WEBSITE

http://www.clairecook.com

READERS' GUIDE

http://www.clairecook.com/author/The_Wildwater_Walking_Club.html

READ-ALIKES

Diamant, Anita. *Good Harbor*—for similar setting and themes.
King, Cassandra. *The Same Sweet Girls*—for similar themes.
Thayer, Nancy. *The Hot Flash Club Chills Out: A Novel*—for similar setting and style.

Sandra Dallas

The Chili Queen

Sandra Dallas earned a degree in journalism from the University of Denver. Following graduation, she worked as a reporter for *Business Week*. She was promoted as the first female bureau chief for the magazine. Dallas has published 10 nonfiction books. She is the recipient of the National Cowboy Hall of Fame Western Heritage Wrangler Award, the Independent Publishers Association Award, and the Ben Franklin Award for her nonfiction. She began publishing fiction in 1990. Her fiction has garnered her much praise, including the Women Writing in the West Willa Award and the Western Writers of America Spur Award. Sandra and her husband Bob live in Denver. They have two grown daughters.

Plot Summary: Addie French is the madam of her very own whorehouse: the Chili Queen. Emma Roby is a mail-order bride on the way to meet her husband in New Mexico. When her groom fails to show, she makes her way to Addie's boarding house. There she meets ex-slave and cook Welcome and Ned, a bank robber in hiding. Ned falls for Emma and soon he, Emma, and Addie are cooking up a scheme that will set them all up to achieve their dreams.

Publication Date: 2002

Number of Pages: 292

Geographic Setting: New Mexico

Time Period: 1860s

Series Notes: This is a stand-alone novel.

Subject Headings: Women—New Mexico—Fiction; Female friendship—Fiction; Boardinghouses—Fiction; New Mexico—Fiction

Appeal Points: Colorful language and engaging characters.

DISCUSSION QUESTIONS

- Several people in the story are harboring secrets. When did you first suspect who Welcome really was?

- Were there any clues in the beginning of the story as to the secrets Emma was hiding?
- Why do you think that Addie is not jealous when she realizes Ned is falling for Emma?
- Given how meek she when we first meet her, are Emma's later actions believable?
- Is there a villain in this story? If so, who do you think it is, and why?

WEBSITE

http://www.sandradallas.com/

READERS' GUIDE

http://media.us.macmillan.com/readersguides/9780312303495RG.pdf

READ-ALIKES

Brennert, Alan. *Honolulu: A Novel*—for similar themes.
Landvik, Lorna. *Oh My Stars*—for similar style and pacing.
Smith, Lee. *Oral History*—for similar style and themes.

Dee Davis

A Match Made on Madison

Dee Davis was born in Texas. She received her bachelor's degree in political science and history and her master's degree in public administration. Before turning to novel writing, she spent 10 years in public relations. In addition, she taught classes at the college level and worked as a lobbyist. Her first novel, *Everything in Its Time*, was published in 2000. Davis is the author of 18 novels and 3 novellas, for which she has won numerous awards.

Though Davis has lived in Austria and Europe, she currently resides in Manhattan with her husband and teenage child.

Plot Summary: Following her apprenticeship to Manhattan matchmaker Althea Sevalas, Vanessa Carlson strikes out to open her own matchmaking business. It is an endeavor that is entirely successful. Soon she is finding love for Manhattan's rich and famous and becoming rivals with her old mentor. The two make a bet: Whoever can marry off multimillionaire property development prince Mark Grayson will be crowned the best Manhattan matchmaker. Crisis after crisis ensues as Vanessa tries to find Mark his Miss Right.

Publication Date: 2007

Number of Pages: 307

Geographic Setting: Manhattan, New York

Time Period: Present day

Series Notes: This is the first book in the Matchmaker Chronicles.

Subject Headings: Dating services—Fiction; Manhattan (New York, N.Y.)—Fiction

Appeal Points: This is a quick, humorous read that will appeal to fans of both romance and chick lit.

DISCUSSION QUESTIONS

- In what ways does Vanessa's story mimic Jane Austen's novel *Emma*?
- In what ways does the author make Manhattan a character in the book? Give some examples.

- When did you first get the idea that Mark was interested in Vanessa? Why do you think it took Vanessa so long to figure it out?
- Have you ever had a rivalry with a friend? How did it affect your friendship?
- Mr. Grayson is used to being in the spotlight. Why do you suppose he is so upset when news of the bet between Vanessa and Althea hits the papers?

WEBSITE

http://www.deedavis.com

READERS' GUIDE

None available.

READ-ALIKES

Kennedy, Erica. *Feminista*—for similar themes and tone.
Trimble, Amanda. *Singletini*—for similar themes and tone.
Weisberger, Lauren. *Chasing Harry Winston*—for similar setting and tone.

Barbara Delinsky

Family Tree

Barbara Delinsky was born on August 9, 1945, in Boston, Massachusetts. She earned her B.A. from Tufts University and an M.A. in sociology from Boston College. Following college, she worked as a researcher for the Massachusetts Society for the Prevention of Cruelty to Children. She has also worked as a newspaper photographer, has done volunteer work, and served on the board of directors of the Friends of the Massachusetts General Hospital Cancer Center and on the MGH's Women's Cancer Advisory Board. In 1980, following the birth of her twins, she turned her attention toward writing. In 1981, her first novel, *The Passionate Touch*, was published by Dell under the name Billie Douglass. She has also published under the name Bonnie Drake. She now publishes solely under the name Barbara Delinsky. There are currently 30 million copies of her titles in print in 25 languages. She currently resides in Newton, Massachusetts, with her husband, Steve Delinsky.

Plot Summary: Loyalty is questioned when a white couple gives birth to a brown-skinned child in a middle-class New England town. Dana and Hugh Clark are thrilled with the birth of their baby girl, but Hugh's family, who can trace their lineage back to the *Mayflower*, are dismayed. Worried over how the birth will affect his writing career, Hugh's father convinces him to go for DNA testing, certain that Dana must have had an affair with their African-American neighbor while Hugh was out of town. The testing proves that Hugh is the father, and the couple set out on a quest to find out where the child's color has come from. Though Dana, who never knew her father, is the suspected culprit, readers will feel a great sense of justice when it is revealed that the African-American blood comes from somewhere in Hugh's family tree. Delinsky has penned a novel that raises questions of racism and the definition of family.

Publication Date: 2007

Number of Pages: 384

Geographic Setting: New England

Time Period: Present day

Series Notes: This is a stand-alone novel.

Subject Headings: Fiction; Fiction/Psychological; Fiction/Sagas; Domestic Fiction; Family—Fiction

Appeal Points: Leisurely-paced, in-depth characters, multiple storylines.

DISCUSSION QUESTIONS

- What do you make of Hugh's reaction in the first few chapters of the novel? Is he racist? Does he believe Dana has had an affair? Is he worried about what his parents and their friends might think?
- How would you react if you found yourself in a situation similar to that of the Clarks? How do you think your friends and family would react?
- How do you feel about Dana's reaction to Hugh's insistence on DNA testing?
- What parallel stories are told throughout the novel?
- Why does Dana hate her father? What did you think about their reunion?
- Dana and Hugh come from very different backgrounds. What do they have in common? What do you think drew them to each other?
- It is said that every family has a closet full of skeletons. Does yours? What makes them secret? How do you think people would react if these secrets were revealed?
- Hugh's family bases a great deal of its identity on its genealogy and the fact that they can trace their ancestry back to the *Mayflower*. Do you think Delinsky's story would have been as effective in other circumstances? What if it had taken place elsewhere? Would the story have changed significantly if two African-American parents had given birth to a primarily white child?

WEBSITE

http://www.barbaradelinsky.com/

READERS' GUIDE

http://www.readinggroupguides.com/guides3/family_tree2.asp

READ-ALIKES

Cleage, Pearl. *Babylon Sisters*—for similar theme of family secrets and search for identity.

Hannah, Kristen. *Summer Island*—for similar leisurely pace and satisfactory conclusion to tribulations. Similar style.

Tyler, Anne. *Digging to America*—for similar themes based on family identity.

Marisa de los Santos

Belong to Me

The first daughter of a surgeon and nurse, Marisa de los Santos grew up in Baltimore, Maryland. She has two children, Charles and Annabel.

Plot Summary: Following a miscarriage, Cornelia Brown and her oncologist husband Tor move from New York City to Philadelphia's suburbs. Cornelia feels out of place in the suburbs. Particularly aggravating is her judgmental neighbor, Piper.

Cornelia forges a friendship with Lake, a waitress who has moved to town from California so that her son can attend a special school for gifted children. Over the course of time, she also learns that there is more to Piper than meets the eye. This once-bitter neighbor drops everything in order to help her best friend who is dying of cancer. Her commitment to her friend earns Cornelia's respect. Soon, secrets are revealed and all three women are forced to deal with harsh realities, which they overcome with aplomb.

Publication Date: 2008

Number of Pages: 400 pages

Geographic Setting: Philadelphia

Time Period: Present day

Series Notes: Cornelia Brown appears in de los Santos' first novel, *Love Walked In*.

Subject Headings: Women—Friendship; Domestic fiction; Contemporary romances; Cancer patients

Appeal Points: Well-drawn characters, multiple plotlines.

DISCUSSION QUESTIONS

- Piper is very critical when she first meets Cornelia. Why do you think she's so critical?

- In what ways do we see Piper develop as a more human character throughout the course of the novel?
- Lake has hidden a great deal from her son. Was she right to try to protect him? Does the end justify the means?
- Discuss Cornelia and Tor's relationship as it evolves throughout the novel.
- Why do you think Cornelia and Dev become friends?
- Piper finds peacefulness in order. Are you someone who thrives on order? Can you think of times in your life when the order you had created was upset? How did you react to that upset?
- How did the events of 9/11 motivate Cornelia and Tor to move to the suburbs?

WEBSITE

http://www.marisadelossantos.com/

READERS' GUIDE

http://www.readinggroupguides.com/guides_b/belong_to_me1.asp

READ-ALIKES

Diamant, Anita. *Good Harbor*—for similar themes and writing style.
Gaffney, Patricia. *The Saving Graces*—for similar themes.
Wingate, Lisa. *The Language of Sycamores*—for similar themes.

Jude Deveraux

Lavender Morning

Jude Deveraux was born Jude Gilliam on September 20, 1947, in Fairdale, Kentucky. She is the oldest of four children. She studied at the Murray State University in Murray, Kentucky. Her first marriage to Mr. White took place in 1967 and ended after just four years. She later married Claude Montassir. The couple adopted a child, Sam Alexander Montassir, who died in a motorcycle accident in 2005. He was eight years old. Deveraux and Montasser subsequently divorced.

Before becoming a writer, she worked as a fifth grade teacher. Her first novel, *The Enchanted Land*, was published in 1977. Deveraux currently divides her time between her homes in North Carolina and Italy.

Plot Summary: Jocelyn Minton's life has been a contradiction. Born to a wealthy socialite and former handyman, she lives happily until her mother passes away and her father returns to his humble roots, marrying a woman with twin daughters of her own. Feeling out of place and unwelcome, Jocelyn finds solace with her elderly neighbor, Miss Edi. When Miss Edi dies, leaving her ancestral manor to Jocelyn, she uncovers instructions and secrets that will bring her to Edilean, Virginia. There, she uncovers a past that has been locked away. She also finds love, though it is not necessarily with the person Miss Edi had planned.

Publication Date: 2009

Number of Pages: 384

Geographic Setting: Virginia

Time Period: Present day

Series Notes: This is the first book in a planned series.

Subject Headings: Inheritance and succession—Fiction; Self-actualization (Psychology)—Fiction

Appeal Points: Detailed, even-paced plot, enjoyable characters, and family secrets.

DISCUSSION QUESTIONS

- Deveraux intertwines two love stories and two time periods. Do you feel she did this successfully?
- Miss Edi's story is one of unrequited love. Have you ever experienced this? Do you feel Miss Edi's actions were convincing?
- Both generations feel the need to find love. Do you believe this to be true of everyone? Do you believe the characters in the novel loved themselves enough?
- Miss Edi has plans for Jocelyn to fall in love and marry Luke. Were you surprised to find her more attracted to Ramsey?
- Do you believe a romance can ultimately survive class differences?

WEBSITE

http://authors.simonandschuster.com/JudeDeveraux/1445134

READERS' GUIDE

None available.

READ-ALIKES

Althouse-Wood, Jill. *Summers at Blue Lake: A Novel of Family Secrets*—for similar themes and pacing.

Miller, Sue. *The World Below*—for similar themes and multidimensional characters.

Shaffer, Louise. *Family Acts: A Novel*—for similar themes.

Anita Diamant

Good Harbor

Anita Diamant was born on June 27, 1951, in New York City. She lived in New Jersey until the age of 12, when her family relocated to Denver, Colorado. She received her B.A. in comparative literature from Washington University. She received her M.A. in English from the State University of New York at Binghamton. Diamant began her writing career in Boston, where she worked as a freelance journalist before publishing her first book, *The New Jewish Wedding*. Her first work of fiction was *The Red Tent*. A historical novel based on the 34th chapter of Genesis, the novel was an immediate word-of-mouth bestseller. Diamant and her husband Bill have one grown daughter. They currently reside in Boston.

Plot Summary: *Good Harbor* is the story of two women, Kathleen Levine and Joyce Tabachnik. The older Kathleen is a wife, mother, grandmother, and children's librarian who has recently been diagnosed with breast cancer. Joyce has just bought a vacation home in the seaside town of Gloucester, Massachusetts. A freelance writer, she hopes to not only vacation there with her family but also write. Troubled by her relationship with her teenage daughter, Joyce, too, is looking for a sympathetic ear. The two women become friends, sharing long walks on Good Harbor Beach, as well as their hopes, dreams, and fears.

Publication Date: 2001

Number of Pages: 288 pages

Geographic Setting: Gloucester, Massachusetts

Time Period: Current day

Series Notes: This is a stand-alone novel.

Subject Headings: Breast cancer patients—Fiction; Jewish women—Fiction; Ann, Cape (Massachusetts)—Fiction

Appeal Points: Lyrical writing, believable characters, humor.

DISCUSSION QUESTIONS

- Anita Diamant does a fabulous job of setting the scene for the story. In what ways has she made Good Harbor Beach a main character in the story?

- Discuss loss and the different ways that the characters in the novel experience it.

- Kathleen converted to Judaism. Joyce considers herself a lapsed Jew. Discuss the ways in which religion affects others in the story.

- Both Joyce and Kathleen crave the conversations of women. Do men converse differently than women? How has the lack of conversation affected the women's relationships with their husbands?

- What do you make of Joyce's reaction to the stature of the Virgin Mary in her yard?

- Does the age difference between Joyce and Kathleen have an effect on their relationship?

WEBSITE

http://www.anitadiamant.com/index.asp?page=home

READERS' GUIDE

http://www.readinggroupguides.com/guides_G/good_harbor1.asp

READ-ALIKES

Delinsky, Barbara. *Coast Road*—for similar themes and style.
Gaffney, Patricia. *The Saving Graces*—for similar themes and style.
Shreve, Anita. *A Wedding in December*—for similar themes.

Susan Donovan

The Kept Woman

Susan Donovan grew up in Milford, Ohio. During high school, she spent a summer in Japan as an exchange student. She attended Northwestern University and graduated in 1983 with a degree in journalism and a minor in Japanese language and sociology.

Prior to writing fiction, Donovan worked as a staff reporter at *The Daily Southtown* in Chicago and did an internship at the *Chicago Tribune*. She also worked for the *Albuquerque Tribune* and the *Indianapolis News*. She married in 1989 and moved to Maryland, where her husband joined a medical practice. There she worked for a U.S. senator, a fine arts fundraiser, and a painted furniture artist. Donovan lives with her husband and two children in rural Maryland.

Plot Summary: Divorcée Samantha Monroe is having a hard time raising her three children on a hairstylist's salary. Jack Tolliver is a politician with a reputation for loving the ladies. When Samantha learns that he is looking for someone to pretend to be his fiancée, she jumps at the chance to make some extra cash. Jack is surprised to find that Samantha is not only pretty but also smart. She is surprised to find he's not quite the cad the rumors would have her believe. Hilarity ensues as the two try to fight their attraction for each other, keep the press from discovering that their engagement is a scam, and deal with Samantha's ex-husband, who is back in town.

Publication Date: 2006

Number of Pages: 372

Geographic Setting: Indianapolis, Indiana

Time Period: Current day

Series Notes: This is a stand-alone novel.

Subject Headings: Single mothers—Fiction; Politicians—Fiction; Divorced women—Fiction; Contemporary romances

Appeal Points: Fast pacing, sexual tension.

DISCUSSION QUESTIONS

- Samantha's husband declared he was gay and left her before her youngest child was even born. What do you think you would do given such a revelation from your spouse?
- Samantha's ex runs off without paying child support. Were you offended by this characterization of him as a gay man? Could Donovan had him do one or the other? Why do you think she chose to present him this way?
- Jack's ex is painted as the anti-hero. Does she have any good qualities? Do you believe she gets her just rewards in the end?
- On the last Friday of every month, Samantha and her friends get together for a "drinks and desperation" night. Do you have a similar ritual with your friends? Do you find it helpful?
- What is Kara's motivation for hooking up Samantha with Jack?
- Would you ever consider being a kept woman?

WEBSITE

http://www.susandonovan.com

READERS' GUIDE

None available.

READ-ALIKES

Bird, Jessica. *An Irresistible Bachelor*—for similar tone, writing style and themes.

Lockwood, Cara. *I Do (But I Don't): A Novel*—for similar tone and style.

Michaels, Kasey. *This Must Be Love*—for similar tone and style.

Sarah Dunn

Secrets to Happiness: A Novel

Sarah Dunn was born in Phoenix, Arizona, on July 28, 1969. She graduated magna cum laude from the University of Pennsylvania, where she majored in English. Following graduation, she wrote a humor column for the *Philadelphia City Paper*. At 24, she published *The Official Slacker Handbook*, which was described as "the '90's answer to *The Preppie Handbook*." Following that publication, she wrote for several television shows, including *Murphy Brown*, *Spin City*, and *Veronica's Closet*. Her first novel, *Big Love*, was published in 2004.

Dunn and her husband, Peter Stevenson, the Executive Editor of *The New York Observer*, live in New York City with their infant son. *Secrets to Happiness* is her second novel.

Plot Summary: Television writer Holly Frick has no luck with men. She's still in love with her ex-husband, an old boyfriend has immortalized their pitiful relationship in a novel, and she is currently involved with a man much younger than herself. Then she meets the boyfriend of her married friend Amanda.

Publication Date: 2009

Number of Pages: 288

Geographic Setting: New York City

Time Period: Present day

Series Notes: This is a stand-alone novel.

Subject Headings: Divorced women—Fiction; New York City—Social life and customs—21st century; Humorous stories; Men–women relations

Appeal Points: Quick pacing, multiple plotlines, humor.

DISCUSSION QUESTIONS

- Do you think Holly overthinks things in her life?
- In what ways does Holly's relationship with her dog change her?

- How does Holly's religious upbringing affect her choices?
- Do you think Holly is too picky when it comes to men?
- Describe Holly's friendship with Leonard. With Amanda.
- How does each character in the novel define happiness? How do you?

WEBSITE

http://www.sarahdunnbooks.com

READERS' GUIDE

http://www.litlovers.com/guide_secrets_to_happiness.html

READ-ALIKES

Alexander, Carly. *Ghosts of Boyfriends Past*—for similar tone and humor.
Green, Jane. *Mr. Maybe*—for similar tone and pacing.
Weiner, Jennifer. *Good in Bed*—for similar tone and pacing.

Joy Fielding

The First Time

Joy Fielding attended the University of Toronto, where she studied theater before receiving her B.A. in English literature. Following graduation, she moved to Los Angeles to pursue a career in acting. She returned to Toronto, where she acted until turning her hand to writing full time. She currently lives in Toronto with her husband and their daughter. The family also has a home in Palm Beach, Florida.

Plot Summary: Mattie Hart has always known that her husband cheats on her. She has found evidence time and time again and has repeatedly disregarded the truth, preferring to leave her world intact. Then the inevitable happens: Jake admits that he has fallen in love with another woman and moves out of the family home. Mattie is torn and her teenage daughter is angry. Then Mattie receives the news that she is dying of Lou Gehrig's disease. Feeling more than a little bit guilty about his bad behavior, Jake moves back home to take care of Mattie, who is now in the awkward position of being cared for by her cheating husband.

Publication Date: 2000

Number of Pages: 352 pages

Geographic Setting: Chicago, Illinois

Time Period: Present day

Series Notes: This is a stand-alone novel.

Subject Headings: Amyotrophic lateral sclerosis—Patients—Fiction; Mothers and daughters—Fiction; Married women—Fiction

Appeal Points: Psychological drama, well-developed characters, satisfying ending.

DISCUSSION QUESTIONS

- Over the years, Mattie destroys the evidence of Jake's affairs. Why do you think she does this? Who is she protecting?

- Do you think Kim ever suspected her father's infidelity?
- Is Kim's reaction to her father's abandonment plausible?
- Why do you think Jake finally decides to do right by Mattie?
- Mattie is put in the position of having to be cared for by someone she does not trust. How would you feel in her position? Would you allow Jake to come back home?
- Describe the relationship between Mattie and Kim.
- In what ways do the relationships between the main characters change over the course of the novel?
- Did you feel it was a believable ending to the story?
- If you were diagnosed with cancer and given only two or three years to live, how would you spend them?

WEBSITE

http://www.joyfielding.com

READERS' GUIDE

None available.

READ-ALIKES

Gould, Judith. *Time to Say Goodbye*—for similar themes.

Frank, Dorothea Benton. *Sullivan's Island: A Lowcountry Tale*—for similar themes.

Haley, Patricia. *No Regrets*—for similar themes and tone.

Lori Foster

Murphy's Law

Lori Foster married her high school sweetheart right out of college. Before having children, she worked as a saleslady, a grocery store clerk, and a handler for Procter & Gamble. She did not turn her hand to writing until her 30s. She completed 10 manuscripts before publishing her first novel, *Impetuous*, with Harlequin in 1996. Since that time, her work has frequently appeared on *The New York Times* and *USA Today* bestseller lists. She received the Career Achievement Award in 2005 from Romantic Times.

Plot Summary: In this sequel to *Jude's Law*, two secondary characters from that novel butt heads as they fall in love. Ashley Miles, a night cleaner who is trying to leave her past behind, finds herself attracted to Quinton Murphy. A 29-year-old virgin, she uses her sarcasm to keep men at bay. Though it has worked on other men, Quinton finds her sassy attitude irresistible. Elements of danger are added into the mix, making for some suspenseful moments before an emotionally satisfying ending.

Publication Date: 2006

Number of Pages: 349

Geographic Setting: Stillbrook, Ohio

Time Period: Present day

Series Notes: This is the second novel in the Law Duology series, following *Jude's Law*.

Subject Headings: Young women—Fiction; Friendship—Fiction; Love stories—American; Romantic suspense stories

Appeal Points: Independent female heroine, suspense, and sexual attraction.

DISCUSSION QUESTIONS

- Ashley is trying to overcome her deadbeat past. What part does that play on her relationships with others, particularly Quinton?

- Do you believe that you can ever truly escape your past?
- In what ways have Ashley's past made her the person she is today?
- Given Ashley's past, is she a reliable narrator?
- Quinton is not put off by Ashley's sassy demeanor. Why? Does their banter add to the sexual tension throughout the novel?
- When Ashley realizes she's in over her head with Quinton, she turns to Denny for advice. Why Denny? What perspective does he offer her?
- Describe the friendship between Ashley and May. Why doesn't Ashley go to May for advice?
- Now that you've finished the novel, will you go back and read *Jude's Law*? Do you feel that you were at a disadvantage not having read that novel first?

WEBSITE

http://www.lorifoster.com/

READERS' GUIDE

None available.

READ-ALIKES

Donovan, Susan. *Knock Me Off My Feet*—for similar style and tone.
Graham, Heather. *Drop Dead Gorgeous*—for similar tone.
Howard, Linda. *Mr. Perfect*—for similar themes and tone.

Karen Joy Fowler

The Jane Austen Book Club

Karen Joy Fowler was born on February 7, 1950, in Bloomington, Indiana. At the age of 11, her father moved the family to Palo Alto, California. She graduated high school in 1968 and went on to get her undergraduate degree in political science from the University of California at Berkley. She received her master's degree at the University of Southern California at Davis. She began writing at the age of 30. Along with writer Pat Murphy, she co-founded the James Tiptree, Jr., Award for fantasy/science fiction works dealing with gender issues. The author currently lives with her husband, Hugh Fowler. The couple has two grown children.

Plot Summary: Fifty-something dog breeder Jocelyn decides to start a book group in which the members only read the novels of Jane Austen. Sylvia, her childhood friend, is agonizing over the recent departure of her husband and her lesbian daughter's move back home. These three women are joined by their friends Bernadette and Prudie, and by one man—Grigg. Grigg is a science fiction reader and new to Austen's work. Over the course of the book club, relationships are tested, new loves are formed, and each member reveals information about her or his innermost self.

Publication Date: 2004

Number of Pages: 304 pages

Geographic Setting: California

Time Period: Present day

Series Notes: This is a stand-alone novel.

Subject Headings: Austen, Jane, 1775–1817—Appreciation—Fiction; Book clubs (discussion groups)—Fiction; Books and reading—Fiction

Appeal Points: Explores social interaction, family dynamics, friendship, and courtship among a group of five well-developed characters.

DISCUSSION QUESTIONS

Note: The novel itself ends with a series of discussion questions, which makes this a good choice for any book group. Consider also the following:

- Discuss the evolution of each book club member.
- What makes Grigg pick up Jane Austen novels? Do you think his observations on the novels discussed are on target?
- Book club members are reading novels written by a woman that deal with women's issues. Do you think their discussions are enhanced by the inclusion of a male in the group? How so?
- Sylvia comments that the issues of most women don't interest most writers. Do you believe that to be a true statement? What authors besides Austen do you think address women's issues well?
- Have you read any of Jane Austen's novels? If not, which would you pick up first, based on the discussions in this book?

WEBSITE

http://www.karenjoyfowler.com

READERS' GUIDE

http://www.readinggroupchoices.com/search/details.cfm?id=17

READ-ALIKES

Monroe, Mary Alice. *The Book Club*—for similar themes and writing style.
Noble, Elizabeth. *The Reading Group*—for similar themes.
Wolitzer, Hilma. *Summer Reading: A Novel*—for similar themes and tone.

Dorothea Benton Frank

Bulls Island

Dorothea Benton Frank was born and raised on Sullivan Island, South Carolina. She is the author of 10 novels. Her work frequently makes *The New York Times* bestseller list. In addition to writing, Frank serves on many charitable boards, including South Carolina Coastal Conservation League and the South Carolina Historical Society.

Frank and her husband, Peter Frank, who have been married for 25 years, have two daughters who attend college in South Carolina. The couple divide their time between New Jersey and South Carolina.

Plot Summary: Twenty years after fleeing her home in Charlottesville, South Carolina, Betts Magee receives an assignment to return home and oversee the development of Bulls Island. It's a fantastic opportunity, one than can either make or break her career. The trouble is, Betts has been living a life of secrets. No one, not even her son Adrian, knows that she's not from Atlanta, or that she has a father, sister and ex-fiancé waiting for her back home. Mistakes made in the past are brought to the surface as two families struggle to work together and overcome their pasts.

Publication Date: 2008

Number of Pages: 352

Geographic Setting: Charlottesville, South Carolina

Time Period: Present day

Series Notes: This is a stand-alone novel.

Subject Headings: Middle-aged women—Fiction; Domestic fiction; South Carolina—Fiction

Appeal Points: Lyrical style, detailed descriptions of setting, and memorable characters.

DISCUSSION QUESTIONS

- Bette has chosen to keep her past a secret from everyone in her life, including her son. Why do you believe she made that decision? Do you think it was the right decision to make at the time?
- Bette does not have a good relationship with her sister. Describe how the two are similar. How are they different?
- How does Bette's relationship with her sister change throughout the course of the novel?
- What is the purpose of the character of Vinnie in the novel? Could the novel have been written without that plotline? How would the ending have differed?
- Betts was J. D. Langley's first love. Despite the passage of time and all that has happened between their two families, they still love each other. Do you remember your first love? Do you believe you can ever go back to that relationship and have it still be the same?
- Why does J. D. put up with his mother's interference?
- How have secrets shaped each of the main characters' lives?
- Describe the mothering styles of both Louisa and Betts. Are they similar in any way?
- The novel is told from two viewpoints, that of Betts and that of J. D. Does this method of storytelling enhance or detract from the novel?

WEBSITE

http://www.dotfrank.com/

READERS' GUIDE

http://www.readinggroupguides.com/guides_B/bulls_island1.asp

READ-ALIKES

Mallery, Susan. *Falling for Gracie*—for similar themes and tone.
Rash, Ron. *Saints at the River*—for similar themes and setting.
Woods, Sherryl. *Feels Like Family*—for similar tone and setting.

Julie Garwood

Fire and Ice

Julie Garwood was born in Kansas, Missouri, in 1946. She is sixth of seven children. Before becoming a novelist, she completed a double major in history and nursing.

Garwood's first novel, *Gentle Warrior*, was released in 1985. To date, she has 15 *New York Times* bestsellers to her credit, with more than 30 million copies of her books in print. In addition to writing romantic suspense novels, she also writes for young adults under the name Emily Chase.

Garwood is married to Gerry Garwood. They have three children and make their home in Leawood, Kansas.

Plot Summary: Sophie Rose is the daughter of a notorious thief, which makes it difficult for her in her role as a big-city crime reporter. When she is assigned to write an expose on her father, she quits her job and goes to work for a small-town paper. There, she writes a story on a runner who later turns up dead in Alaska with her business card tucked into one of his socks. Sophie convinces her boss to let her travel to Alaska to investigate the runner's death. While there, she finds herself the target of a killer who does not want a conspiracy revealed. Passion ensues between Sophie and Jack MacAlister, the bodyguard who is assigned to protect her.

Publication Date: 2008

Number of Pages: 352

Geographic Setting: Chicago and Alaska

Time Period: Present day

Series Notes: This is a stand-alone novel, though the main character first appears in *Murder List*.

Subject Headings: Journalists—Fiction; Bodyguards—Fiction; Chicago (Illinois)—Fiction; Prudhoe Bay (Alaska)—Fiction

Appeal Points: Quirky heroine, romantic suspense, humor, and strong characters.

DISCUSSION QUESTIONS

- Why do you suppose Sophie and Jack fight their attraction?
- Describe Sophie's relationship with Herman Bitterman. Have you ever had a boss who was also a parent figure to you?
- Sophie tries very hard to distinguish herself as separate from her father. Do you believe one can ever truly escape her or his familial past?
- Sophie also appears in *Murder List*. Have you read that novel? Is her character in *Fire and Ice* consistent with the former novel?
- Many of Garwood's characters show up in later novels. Is there a character from this book that you would like to appear in a future book? Why?

WEBSITE

http://www.juliegarwood.com

READERS' GUIDE

None available.

READ-ALIKES

Howard, Linda. *Burn: A Novel*—for fast-paced dialogue, romantic suspense, and quirky characters.

Robards, Karen. *Obsession*—for similar pacing, romantic suspense mixed with humor, and well-developed characters.

Robb, J. D. Eve Dallas *In Death* series—for witty dialogue, suspense, and pacing.

Whitney Gaskell

Mommy Tracked

Whitney Gaskell was born in 1972 and grew up in Syracuse, New York. She is a graduate of Tulane Law School. Her first novel, *Pushing 30*, was published in 2003. Gaskell also writes young adult fiction under the pen name Piper Banks. She lives with her husband, George Gaskell, and their son in Florida.

Plot Summary: MCT (Mothers Coming Together) is a group of women in Orange Cove, Florida, formed to support each other and have some time away from home. Its four members include Anna Swann, Grace Weaver, Juliet Cole, and Chloe Truman. Anna is a single mother and restaurant critic. Grace is the married other of three. Juliet is a successful attorney as well as the mother of twins. Chloe Truman, who goes into labor at a neighborhood party, is the newest member of the group. Each woman has a problem she needs to overcome. The friends help each other in unexpected ways, adding humor as they go along.

Publication Date: 2007

Number of Pages: 349

Geographic Setting: Orange Grove, Florida

Time Period: Present day

Series Notes: This is a stand-alone novel.

Subject Headings: Married women—Fiction; Single women—Fiction; Female friendship—Fiction

Appeal Points: Female friendship, humor, fast pacing, and multiple storylines.

DISCUSSION QUESTIONS

- There was a time when women had to choose between a family and a career. Today, many women choose both. Do you think it was harder for women then than it is today? In what way?

- Did you identify with any particular character? Which one and why?
- Each of the four women suffers from insecurities. What are they insecure about and how does that manifest itself in each of their lives?
- The novel takes place in suburbia. Would it have rung true had it been set elsewhere?
- Each chapter in the novel focuses on one woman. Did this make the transition from chapter to chapter difficult for you? Why do you suppose the author did this?

WEBSITE

http://www.whitneygaskell.com

READERS' GUIDE

http://www.readinggroupguides.com/guides_M/mommy_tracked1.asp

READ-ALIKES

Thayer, Nancy. *The Hot Flash Club*—for similar themes, pacing, and tone.

Valdes-Rodriguez, Alisa. *The Dirty Girls Social Club*—for similar themes, pacing, and tone.

Wells, Rebecca. *Ya-Yas in Bloom*—for similar themes.

Emily Giffin

Something Borrowed

Emily Fisk Giffin was born on March 20, 1972. In 1986, her family moved to Naperville, Illinois, where she attended high school. She graduated in 1990. Emily graduated from Wake Forest University in 1994 with a double major in history and English. She went on to receive her J.D. from the University of Virginia law school. Following her graduation, she moved to Manhattan and began working in the litigation department at Winston & Strawn. Five days after the tragic events of 9/11, Emily quit her job and moved to London, where she began writing *Something Borrowed* under its original name, *Rolling the Dice*. She signed a two book contract with St. Martin's Press in 2002, which published *Something Borrowed* in 2004. That novel has since been made into a feature film starring Kate Hudson, Ginnifer Goodwin and Colin Eggesfield.

Emily and her husband are the parents of twin boys, Edward and George, and a daughter, Harriet. The family resides in London.

Plot Summary: Young Manhattan attorney Rachel turns 30 and sleeps with her best friend's fiancé, Dex. Rachel is dutifully appalled at her behavior and vows to put the whole mess behind her, but Cupid has other plans as the wedding approaches and Rachel and Dex find that they can't fight their attraction to each other.

Publication Date: 2004

Number of Pages: 336 pages

Geographic Setting: Manhattan, New York City

Time Period: Present day

Series Notes: This is a stand-alone novel.

Subject Headings: Triangles (interpersonal relations)—Fiction; Female friendship—Fiction; Single women—Fiction; Chick Lit

Appeal Points: Fast pace and humor, with enjoyable characters.

DISCUSSION QUESTIONS

- Discuss Rachel and Darcy's friendship. Is there anything genuine about it? Has it deteriorated over time?
- Do you believe that Rachel's indiscretion with Dex was truly an accident?
- Discuss whether it is ever acceptable to cheat with a friend's boyfriend.
- Giffin puts Rachel in a situation that makes her look unsympathetic to the reader. Yet she is the main character of the story. Did Rachel win you over?
- If Dex had not met Rachel, do you believe he would have gone through with the wedding?
- Who were you rooting for in the story?
- We get the story from Rachel's perspective. Do you think the story would have been told differently from Darcy's point of view? From Dex's?

WEBSITE

http://www.emilygiffin.com/

READERS' GUIDE

http://www.emilygiffin.com/books/somethingborrowed_guide.php

READ-ALIKES

Ahearn, Cecelia. *Rosie Dunne*—for similar tone and writing style.
Green, Jane. *To Have and to Hold*—for similar themes and style.
Markham, Wendy. *Slightly Married*—for similar themes and tone.

Julia Glass

I See You Everywhere

Julia Glass was born March 23, 1956, in Boston, Massachusetts. She received her B.A. from Yale University in 1978. Following graduation, she moved to New York City to paint and supported herself as a copy editor for *Cosmopolitan* magazine. Glass currently resides in Marblehead, Massachusetts, with her partner, Dennis Cowley, and their two children. Glass is the 2002 winner of the National Book Award for her debut novel, *Three Junes*.

Plot Summary: *I See You Everywhere* is the story of two sisters, polar opposites, who reconnect after a long absence at the home of their recently deceased great-great aunt in Vermont. It is also the story of the people who populate their lives over the years.

Publication Date: 2008

Number of Pages: 304

Geographic Setting: Vermont, Rhode Island, Manhattan, Rocky Mountains

Time Period: Present day

Series Notes: This is a stand-alone novel.

Subject Headings: Sisters—Fiction; Domestic fiction; Interpersonal relations

Appeal Points: Familial relationships, hidden secrets, with witty dialogue.

DISCUSSION QUESTIONS

- If you have read Glass's novel *Three Junes*, does the mother in this novel remind you of the mother in that novel?
- Clem is a biologist interested in endangered species. Do you believe there is anything we can do to protect the world we live in?

- The same woman raised both daughters. Why do you think Louisa turned out so predictable and settled while Clem turned out to be so adventurous?
- Do you have siblings? Are you very different? In what ways are you similar?
- In what ways are the sisters similar?
- Although the two sisters are very different, their relationship is based on affection. In what ways does this affection manifest itself?
- Discuss the effects of family closeness on each of the characters in the novel.

WEBSITE

Glass does not have a website.

READERS' GUIDE

None available.

READ-ALIKES

Arnold, Elizabeth Joy. *Pieces of My Sister's Life*—for similar themes.
Brown, Rita Mae. *Six of One*—for similar themes.
Picoult, Jodi. *My Sister's Keeper*—for similar themes and style.

Eileen Goudge

Domestic Affairs

Eileen Goudge was born on July 4, 1950. One of six children, she grew up on the San Francisco Bay area. Her first writing break came in the 80s when she was hired to help launch the successful *Sweet Valley High* series. Her first adult novel, *Garden of Lies*, was published in 1986. After three divorces and two children, she has finally found love. She is now married to Sandy Kenyon, a radio talk show host who formerly worked for CNN. The couple resides in New York City.

Plot Summary: Abigail and Lila were best friends. Lila came from a wealthy family. Abigail's mother was their housekeeper. The girls were as close as any two children could be, until Abigail's mother was accused of stealing and she and Abigail were ejected from the household. In a shocking turn of events, Abigail grows up to be a popular chef with a published cookbook. She and her husband are happily raising their daughter. On the other hand, Lila has lost not only her factory in a fire but also her husband to suicide. She shows up on Abigail's doorstop, begging for a job and is hired as—you guessed it, their housekeeper.

Publication Date: 2008

Number of Pages: 437

Geographic Setting: Georgia

Time Period: 1982 to present

Series Notes: This is a stand-alone novel.

Subject Headings: Housekeepers—Fiction; Women friends—Fiction

Appeal Points: Domestic fiction, women's friendships, and well-drawn characters.

DISCUSSION QUESTIONS

- Abigail dreams of revenge but is unable to savor it when Lila reappears in her life after suffering terrible losses. Can revenge ever be sweet?

- Do you believe in the old adage "What goes around comes around?"
- If you were betrayed by a friend, would you be able to forgive her or him?
- Discuss the relationship between Lila and Concepcíon.
- Discuss the relationship between Abigail and her husband. How do her memories of Vaughn effect that relationship?

WEBSITE

http://www.eileengoudge.net/

READERS' GUIDE

http://www.readinggroupguides.com/guides_d/domestic_affairs1.asp

READ-ALIKES

Koomson, Dorothy. *My Best Friend's Girl*—for similar themes.
Noble, Elizabeth M. *The Friendship Test*—for similar themes.
Siddons, Anne Rivers. *Outer Banks: A Novel*—for similar themes and writing style.

Jane Green

The Other Woman

Jane Green Warburg was born in London on May 31, 1968. She attended the University of Wales at Aberystwyth. Following graduation, she worked in entertainment journalism, eventually working her way up to feature writer at *The Daily Express* in London. Her first novel, *Straight Talking*, was published in 1995. Green is one of the founders of the chick lit genre. She currently lives in Westport, Connecticut, with her husband Ian Warburg and their six children.

Plot Summary: Dan is everything that Ellie is not. She has longed for a mother and doting family and is thrilled when welcomed into the Cooper family. Little by little, she comes to discover that her fiancé is a mama's boy. Linda Cooper has suddenly taken over Ellie's life, including her wedding plans. What was meant to be a cozy ceremony with close friends has begun to turn into a three-ring-circus. To make it worse, Dan seems to be on his mother's side. When Ellie learns that she is pregnant, her relationship with her mother-in-law starts to go from bad to worse.

Publication Date: 2005

Number of Pages: 389

Geographic Setting: England

Time Period: Present day

Series Notes: This is a stand-alone novel.

Subject Headings: Triangles (interpersonal relations)—Fiction; Mothers-in-law—Fiction; Married women—Fiction

Appeal Points: Authentic heroines, witty dialogue, and serious situations mixed with humor.

DISCUSSION QUESTIONS

- How does Emma grow as an individual throughout the course of the novel?

- Does Linda have any redeeming qualities?
- Why do you suppose it takes so long for Dan to stick up for Emma? Did you feel this was a foreshadowing of things to come? What do you imagine happens to Dan and Emma after the novel ends?
- Have you ever wished for a family larger/smaller; closer/more distant than your own? Do you suppose that is typical?
- Is Linda a stereotype? How is your own relationship with your mother-in-law?
- Why do you suppose Ellie never stands up for herself?

WEBSITE

http://www.janegreen.com

READERS' GUIDE

http://www.readinggroupguides.com/guides3/the_other_woman1.asp

READ-ALIKES

Cabot, Meg. *Queen of Babble*—for witty dialogue, humor, and similar themes.

Delinsky, Barbara. *Family Tree*—for character-driven plotline and writing style.

Weiner, Jennifer. *Best Friends Forever*—for character-driven plotline and writing style.

Kristin Hannah

Firefly Lane

Kristen Hannah was born in Garden Grove, California, on September 25, 1960. When she was 8, the family moved to Western Washington. Before completing her J.D. at the University of Puget Sound, she worked for an advertising agency. Her first novel, *A Hand Full of Heaven*, was published in 1991. She now has 18 novels to her credit. *Firefly Lane* was on *The New York Times* bestseller list for eight and a half months in 2009. Hannah and her husband reside in Washington State with their children.

Plot Summary: Despite their many differences, Kate Mularkey and Tully Hart become fast friends when the latter moves into the neighborhood in 1974. Their friendship spans the years to adulthood, when Kate becomes a housewife and mother and Tully's ambition takes her to New York and the world of television journalism. Jealousy threatens their friendship, which faces the ultimate test following a betrayal.

Publication Date: 2008

Number of Pages: 479

Geographic Setting: Seattle, Washington

Time Period: 1970s–Present

Series Notes: This is a stand-alone novel.

Subject Headings: Best Friends—Fiction; Friendship in adolescence—Fiction; Female friendship—Fiction

Appeal Points: Family relationships, secrets, loss, and coming of age make this a tearjerker.

DISCUSSION QUESTIONS

- How has motherhood changed Kate? Has she lost sight of who she once wanted to be?

- Tully seems to have everything, yet she is lonely. Why?
- Discuss Tully's relationship with her mother. What about Kate's relationship with Marah? Why do you believe Tully gets so close to Marah?
- How much of our upbringing determines who we are as adults?
- Have you ever felt jealousy for a friend? How did you come to terms with it? Did it ruin your friendship?
- Do you believe that there are some betrayals that are unforgiveable?

WEBSITE

http://www.kristinhannah.com

READERS' GUIDE

http://www.kristinhannah.com/content/book_clubs.php

READ-ALIKES

Delinsky, Barbara. *While My Sister Sleeps*—for similar themes of jealousy, coming of age, and similar tone.

Rice, Luanne. *Firefly Beach*—for similar tone, familial relationships, and coming-of-age themes.

Wolitzer, Meg. *The Ten-Year Nap*—for similar tone and troubled characters.

Jane Heller

Female Intelligence

Jane Heller grew up one of six children in Scarsdale, New York. She received her B.A. in classics from Rochester University. She received her master's in communication from Pennsylvania's Annenberg School of Communications. Heller worked in publishing for a decade before turning to writing. Her first novel, *Cha Cha Cha*, was published by Kensington in 1994. She now has 13 novels and one nonfiction book to her credit. Many of her novels have been optioned for film. Heller and her husband make their home in Santa Barbara, California.

Plot Summary: Lynne Wyman has gotten famous for her nationally known Wyman Method in which she conducts seminars teaching men how to speak to women. She is on top of the world until she learns of her husband's infidelity and their break-up is leaked to the media. Suddenly, she is no longer credible. What is a girl to do? She quickly hatches a plan to turn Brandon Brock, "America's Toughest Boss," into the most sensitive one. Hilarity ensues as she tries to form Brock to her mold while ultimately falling for him.

Publication Date: 2001

Number of Pages: 335

Geographic Setting: New York City

Time Period: Present day

Series Notes: This is a stand-alone novel.

Subject Headings: Women linguists—Fiction; Interpersonal communication—Fiction; New York (New York)—Fiction; Sensitivity training—Fiction; Chick lit

Appeal Points: Romantic comedy, humor, and strong female characters.

DISCUSSION QUESTIONS

- Is there a difference between what women say and think and what is best for them? How is this true in the novel?

- Do men and women speak different languages? Why do you think books like *Men Are from Mars, Women Are from Venus* are so popular?
- How do Lynn's friends support her throughout the novel?
- Did you find the novel sexist in any way? What if the main character had been a male trying to teach women how to speak to men?

WEBSITE

http://www.janeheller.com

READERS' GUIDE

None available.

READ-ALIKES

Brodeur, Adrienne. *Man Camp: A Novel*—for similar themes and tone.
Curyn, Lynda. *Engaging Men*—for humor, characterization, and pacing.
Krum, Sharon. *The First Thing about Jane Spring: A Novel*—for similar themes and tone.

Judi R. Hendricks

The Baker's Apprentice

Hendricks was born one of two children in Silicon Valley. The family moved often. She received her B.A. in journalism. Before trying her hand at writing, she worked as a journalist, substitute teacher, in advertising and travel, and as a baker. She finally attended a writing seminar at the University of California at Irvine. Her first novel, *Bread Alone*, was published in 2001. Hendricks and her husband, Geoff, now reside in Santa Fe, New Mexico.

Plot Summary: Former Los Angeles socialite Wynter Morrison is now a full partner at the Queen Street Bakery. Financially strapped, she is waiting for her divorce settlement to come through. Things are not all that rosy between Wynter and her writer boyfriend Mack either, especially when he up and travels to Alaska, hoping to cure his writer's block.

Publication Date: 2005

Number of Pages: 372

Geographic Setting: Seattle, Washington, and Yukon, Alaska

Time Period: Present day

Series Notes: Sequel to *Bread Alone*.

Subject Headings: Divorced women—Fiction; Bakers—Fiction; Baking—Fiction; Seattle (Washington)—Fiction

Appeal Points: Leisurely pace and rich description.

DISCUSSION QUESTIONS

- Why does Mack have such trouble talking about his childhood?
- How does Tyler change over the course of the novel? What propels this change?
- In what ways does Wynter create a family for herself in Seattle?

- How is the bakery a character in the story? Give examples.
- Would you expect yourself, in Wynter's position, to have trouble trusting men again?

WEBSITE

http://www.judihendricks.com

READERS' GUIDE

None available.

READ-ALIKES

Bretton, Barbara. *Just Desserts*—for similar themes and characters.
Kirchner, Bharti. *Pastries: A Novel of Desserts and Discoveries*—for similar pace and lush descriptions.
Lynch, Sarah-Kate. *By Bread Alone*—for similar themes and tone.

Patti Callahan Henry

The Art of Keeping Secrets

Patti Callahan Henry grew up as a minister's daughter and was taught the importance of storytelling from her father. She attended Auburn University in Montgomery, Alabama, and received a master's degree in child heath. Before becoming a full-time writer, Henry worked as a clinical nurse specialist. Her first novel, *Losing the Moon*, was published in 2004. To date, she is the author of six *New York Times* bestselling novels. Henry, her husband, and three children live just outside Atlanta on the Chattahoochee River.

Plot Summary: Amy Reynolds and Nick Lowry were college sweethearts who parted when Nick traveled to Costa Rica on a conservation program. Amy went on with her life, married, had children, and settled into a comfortable, domestic life. Things change abruptly when Amy's son, Jack, asks his parents to meet the parents of his girlfriend, Lisbeth. Lisbeth's father turns out to be none other than Nick Lowry. An avid conservationist, Nick joins Amy on her quest to save a historic plantation. Sparks are soon reignited as the two begin to spend more time with each other than with their families.

Publication Date: 2004

Number of Pages: 365

Geographic Setting: Georgia

Time Period: Present day

Series Notes: This is a stand-alone novel.

Subject Headings: Women college teachers—Fiction; Parent and adult child—Fiction; Middle-aged women—Fiction; Married women—Fiction; First loves—Fiction

Appeal Points: Lyrical dialogue, detailed descriptions, and a character-driven plot.

DISCUSSION QUESTIONS

- Think about your first true love. Have you ever gotten over that relationship? How do you think you would react if you were to see him again?

- What options were possible for Amy and Nick? Do you think they chose the right option?
- Amy's affair comes as her children are moving on. It has often been said that this is a delicate time, when spouses either redefine their marriages and find a renewed pleasure in each other or move on. Have you dealt with these feelings? Do you think Amy would have made the same choices had her children still been small?
- Both Amy and Nick have fallen into passive roles in their lives. Do you think that is inevitable in our lives? Do you ever think about the "road not taken?"
- Discuss Amy and Nick's spouses. How did you feel about them as characters in the novel?

WEBSITE

http://www.patticallahanhenry.com

READERS' GUIDE

http://www.patticallahanhenry.com/PDF/LosingtheMoonGuide.pdf

READ-ALIKES

Gaffney, Patricia. *The Saving Graces*—for lyrical dialogue and character-driven storyline.

Hoffman, Alice. *Here on Earth*—for similar themes and character-driven storyline.

Monroe, Mary Alice. *The Beach House*—for lyrical dialogue, Southern setting, and similar themes.

Elin Hilderbrand

A Summer Affair: A Novel

Elin Hilderbrand grew up in Collegeville, Pennsylvania. She is a graduate of both John Hopkins University and the University of Iowa's Graduate Fiction Workshop. Her first novel, *The Beach Club*, was published in 2000. She now has 10 novels to her credit. Hilderbrand, her husband, and their three children reside in Nantucket.

Plot Summary: Glassblower Claire Danner Crispin is about as Irish Catholic as one can get. She gave up working full time in order to be the perfect wife and mother of four. She is asked by Locke Dixon to co-chair the Nantucket Children's Summer Gala and to also create an original piece of glasswork for the program. Claire agrees because she feels guilt over the fact that Locke's wife got hurt one evening when out drinking with Claire and her friends. Soon, the two begin an intense affair, causing Claire to question all of the choices she has made in her life.

Publication Date: 2008

Number of Pages: 408

Geographic Setting: Nantucket Island, Massachusetts

Time Period: Present day

Series Notes: This is a stand-alone novel.

Subject Headings: Single mothers—Fiction; Women glassworkers—Fiction; Parties—Fiction; Fundraising—Fiction; Nantucket Island (Massachusetts)—Fiction

Appeal Points: Rich descriptions, leisurely pace, and multiple viewpoints.

DISCUSSION QUESTIONS

- Claire feels overwhelmed with her responsibilities as an artist, wife, mother, and co-chair. Do you believe these are sufficient enough reasons to cause her to have an affair? Are women today overburdened with responsibility?

- What situations allow Locke to pursue an affair with Claire?
- Why do you suppose Jason is so bitter about Claire's art? Did Claire make a mistake in allowing his feelings about her career to dictate her life?
- Have you ever felt the need to say yes and take on more than you could handle? What do you think makes women so willing to do this?
- The novel is rich in descriptive setting. Discuss how the island of Nantucket is a character in the novel.

WEBSITE

http://elinhilderbrand.net/

READERS' GUIDE

http://www.readinggroupguides.com/guides_s/a_summer_affair1.asp

READ-ALIKES

Berg, Elizabeth. *Talk Before Sleep: A Novel*—for pacing and similar theme of self-realization.

Frank, Dorothea Benton. *The Land of Mango Sunsets: A Novel*—for similar pacing, descriptions, and themes.

Mattison, Alice. *The Wedding of the Two-headed Woman*—for similar themes and tone.

Cathy Holton

Beach Trip: A Novel

Cathy Holton grew up in North Carolina in the 1960s. She is the author of three novels, all published by Ballantine/Random House Books. Holton lives in Chattanooga, Tennessee, with her husband and three children.

Plot Summary: Twenty-three years after graduating from college, four friends reunite at the beach on Whale Head Island in North Carolina. Mel, Sara, Annie, and Lola have each followed different paths following their four years spent together. Lola, married to a very wealthy and successful man, pops pills to deal with his indifferent behavior toward her. Mel, an author living in New York, has two failed marriages to her credit. Sara is dealing with her son's illness, and Annie is contemplating an affair. Over the course of the week, all of the women reveal their personal struggles, inevitably reliving their pasts and leaning on each other for the strength they need to face their futures head on.

Publication Date: 2009

Number of Pages: 432

Geographic Setting: Outer Banks, North Carolina

Time Period: 1980s to 2005

Series Notes: This is a stand-alone novel.

Subject Headings: Female friendship—Fiction; Reunions—Fiction; Women college graduates—Fiction; Outer Banks (North Carolina)—Fiction

Appeal Points: Dark humor, middle-aged women coming of age, and multiple points of view.

DISCUSSION QUESTIONS

- Mel, Sara, Annie, and Lola grew up in the South. Did this affect their lives and what they became in any way? Do you think the novel would have read differently had the women grown up in the North?

- Given the title of the novel and the front cover, were you surprised by the depth of the characters and tone of the writing? Think of an alternate title for the novel. What would it be?
- The novel moves back and forth from the past to the present. Did you find this irksome? Why do you think the novelist chose to reveal the past in flashbacks?
- Of the four women, Mel is the one who is the most independent. She has married and divorced twice. Do you believe she is commitment phobic? Why or why not?
- Which character did you most identify with? Which character was your least favorite?

WEBSITE

http://www.cathyholton.com

READERS' GUIDE

None available.

READ-ALIKES

Goudge, Eileen. *Immediate Family*—for similar themes.
King, Cassandra. *The Same Sweet Girls*—for similar themes and tone.
Smith, Lee. *The Last Girls: A Novel*—for similar themes.

Ann Hood

The Knitting Circle

Ann Hood was born in 1956 in West Warwick, Rhode Island. She received B.A. in English from the University of Rhode Island. She attended graduate school at New York University, where she studied American literature. Her first novel, *Somewhere off the Coast of Maine*, was published while she was working as a flight attendant for TWA. Since then, she has published eight novels, a book of nonfiction on the art of writing, and a collection of short stories. She has won a Best American Spiritual Writing Award, the Paul Bowles Prize for Short Fiction, and two Pushcart Prizes. In 2002, Hood's 5-year-old Grace died suddenly. She has since adopted and now lives in Providence, Rhode Island, with her husband and two children, Sam and Annabelle.

Plot Summary: Like Mary Baxter, the protagonist of this novel, Ann Hood learned to knit while grieving over the loss of her daughter. Struggling to save her marriage in the face of such tragedy and unable to focus on work, Mary joins a knitting circle at the urging of her mother, now living in Mexico. At first, Mary is unwilling to open up to the women in her group. One by one, each woman teaches her a different knitting technique and, in so doing, also reveals her story. Mary is eventually able to reveal her own hurt and begin rebuilding her life.

Publication Date: 2007

Number of Pages: 384

Geographic Setting: Providence, Rhode Island

Time Period: Present day

Series Notes: This is a stand-alone novel.

Subject Headings: Women—Friendship; Knitting—Therapeutic use; Mother and daughter; Family relationships; Grief in women

Appeal Points: Believable characters, exploration of the stages of grief, strong development of supporting characters.

DISCUSSION QUESTIONS

- Knitting is well known to be therapeutic. What makes it so?
- Discuss the stages of grief that Mary goes through. How is each stage characterized?
- During times of grief, some people reach out for the comfort of others. Some withdraw into themselves. Mary's tendency is to avoid the discussion of difficult issues. What is your tendency when dealing with difficulties? What is the appeal of that choice?
- Each woman in the knitting circle has experienced a loss in her life. How are their losses similar? In what ways are they unique?
- Does Mary's difficult relationship with her mother influence the way in which she deals with her grief over the loss of Stella?
- Describe the changes in Mary and Dylan's relationship over the course of the novel.
- Explore Mary's relationship with her mother. Is Mary in any way responsible for her mother's reluctance to be open with her?

WEBSITE

http://www.annhood.us/

READERS' GUIDE

http://books.wwnorton.com/books/ReadingGuidesDetail.aspx?ID=13751&CID=8278&tid=3288&tcid=:

READ-ALIKES

Jacob, Kathleen. *Friday Night Knitting Circle*—similar themes.
Kelly, Kathy. *Just Between Us*—similar style of character.
Macomber, Debbie. *Back on Blossom Street*—similar themes.

Kate Jacobs

The Friday Night Knitting Club

Kate Jacobs grew up in a small town in Vancouver, British Columbia. She attended boarding school in Victoria, B.C., and received her B.A. in journalism from Carleton University in Ottawa. She received her master's degree from New York University. Following graduation, she worked as an assistant to the book and fiction editor at *Redbook* magazine. She worked as an editor at *Working Women* and *Family Life* and later as a writer and editor for Lifetime Television's website. Her first novel, *A Sister's Wish*, was published in 1995. In 2007, she published *The Friday Night Knitting Club*, launching a well-loved series. Kate, her husband, and their English springer spaniel now reside in Southern California.

Plot Summary: Georgia Walker is busy running her Manhattan yarn shop and raising her 12-year-old daughter Dakota on her own. She is aided by her employees and the friends she makes at the new knitting club she starts at her shop. Each woman has a story to unfold. As they do, Georgia begins to open up herself, revealing a painful past and beginning to let herself trust these women. Old wounds are reopened and a tragedy strikes before the book closes, leaving questions unanswered and opening the door to the novel's sequel.

Publication Date: 2007

Number of Pages: 345

Geographic Setting: Manhattan, New York, and Scotland

Time Period: Present day

Series Notes: This is the first novel in Jacob's Knitting Club series.

Subject Headings: Mothers and daughters—Fiction; Female friendship—Fiction; Knitters (persons)—Fiction; Knitting—Fiction; New York (New York)—Fiction

Appeal Points: Likeable characters, plot twists, breezy style, even pace, women's friendships, and overcoming loss.

DISCUSSION QUESTIONS

- How does Jacobs use knitting as a metaphor for life? Give some examples.
- How do you suppose Georgia's past in rural Pennsylvania informs the woman she becomes as an adult? In what ways has she been betrayed by those she loved?
- Which character do you most relate to? Why? Do you feel that any of the characters were underdeveloped?
- Did you believe that James would behave the way he does when he returns to Georgia?
- Dakota is biracial. Do you believe James when he says that he has things to teach her that Georgia cannot impart? Do you think racial diversity in a family matters?
- What do you suppose will happen to Dakota after the book ends?

WEBSITE

http://www.katejacobsbooks.com/

READERS' GUIDE

http://www.katejacobsbooks.com/fnkc_readguide.html

READ-ALIKES

Harbison, Elizabeth M. *Shoe Addicts Anonymous*—for similar themes and tone.
LaZebnik, Claire Scovell. *Knitting under the Influence*—for similar themes.
Macomber, Debbie. *A Good Yarn*—for similar themes and tone.

Brenda Janowitz

Scot on the Rocks: How I Survived My Ex-boyfriend's Wedding with My Dignity Ever-so Slightly Intact

Brenda Janowitz attended Cornell University where she received her B.S. in human service studies with a concentration in race and discrimination. Following college, she attended Hofstra Law School where she was a member of the Law Review and won the Law Review Writing Competition. She passed the bar and worked first as a lawyer and then as a federal clerk. She has been a career counselor at two New York City law schools. Janowitz currently lives in New York City with her husband and teaches creative writing at Mediabistro. *Scot on the Rocks* is her debut novel.

Plot Summary: Successful Manhattan attorney Brooke Miller is living with handsome Scotsman Douglas when she receives an invitation to attend her ex-boyfriend Trip's wedding to an L.A. starlet. She accepts the invitation, planning to introduce Douglas as her fiancé—a plan that is ruined when he dumps her days before the wedding. What is Brooke to do? She convinces her co-worker Jack to pretend to be Douglas at the wedding. As one might expect, hilarity ensues.

Publication Date: 2007

Number of Pages: 295

Geographic Setting: New York City

Time Period: Present day

Series Notes: This is the first in the Brooke Miller series.

Subject Headings: Women lawyers; Dating (social customs); Self-fulfillment in women; New York City; Chick lit

Appeal Points: This is a humorous, quick read with likeable characters.

DISCUSSION QUESTIONS

- Have you ever been invited to an ex-boyfriend's wedding? If not, think back to how you felt when hearing the news of an ex's upcoming nuptials. How did you feel? Were you happy, sad, or jealous?
- Brooke has put Trip and his family on a pedestal in her memory. What unfolds to make her change her mind?
- Why do Brooke and Jack try to avoid their attraction to each other? Have you ever dated a coworker? Why do you think so many companies discourage or forbid intra-office dating?
- Why does Jack go along with Brooke's request to attend the wedding?
- Do you think Brooke and Jack's relationship will last?

WEBSITE

http://www.brendajanowitz.com/

READERS' GUIDE

http://www.brendajanowitz.com/books_club_scot.html
http://www.readinggroupguides.com/guides_S/scot_on_the_rocks1.asp

READ-ALIKES

Curnyn, Lynda. *Bombshell*—for similar tone.
Hopkins, Christina. *Cyber Cinderella*—for similar writing style and tone.
Young, Elizabeth. *The Wedding Date*—for similar storyline.

Janice Kaplan

The Botox Diaries

Janice Kaplan graduated magna cum laude from Yale University and won that institution's Murray Fellowship for writing. She began her career as an on-air sports reporter for CBS radio. Since that time, she has worked as a columnist for *Seventeen* magazine; deputy editor of *TV Guide* magazine and executive director of the TV Guide Television Group; and as a producer for ABC's *Good Morning America*. She is currently the editor at *Parade* magazine. Kaplan is also the author and co-author of 11 books. Kaplan lives with her husband in Larchmont, New York. She has two sons who are currently attending Yale.

Plot Summary: Jess and Lucy are 40-somethings living in New York City. Jess is divorced from her cheating French husband and is raising her daughter alone while working at the Arts Council for Kids. When she is not dealing with the spoiled, rich mothers of the children she works with, she's being set up by her best friend Lucy, attending Botox parties, and fending off her ex-husband, who has suddenly returned. Lucy, for her part, is having an extra-marital affair, leaving Jess feeling torn between Lucy and her husband, who she is also very close to. This is great chick lit for middle-aged women.

Publication Date: 2004

Number of Pages: 296

Geographic Setting: Manhattan and California

Time Period: Present day

Series Notes: This is a stand-alone novel.

Subject Headings: Middle-aged women—Fiction; Female friendship—Fiction; Midlife crisis—Fiction; Love triangles—Fiction

Appeal Points: Humor.

DISCUSSION QUESTIONS

- Jess is having a difficult time with the fact that her daughter is growing up. Do you think this is true of all mothers? Do you think single mothers have a harder time letting go?
- Why do you think Jess allows Lucy to buy her cooperation in her affair?
- If your husband cheated on you, would you ever consider taking him back? Do you think Jess makes the right decision with regard to Jacques?
- Why do you think Lucy has an affair? Do you think an affair can ever be condoned?
- The novel takes place in New York City and most of the characters are wealthy women. Do you think the story would make sense had it been set elsewhere? Why or why not?

WEBSITE

http://www.janicekaplan.com/

READERS' GUIDE

None available.

READ-ALIKES

Heller, Jane. *An Ex to Grind*—for similar writing style and tone.

Satran, Pamela Redmond. *The Man I Should Have Married*—for similar themes, setting and humor.

Skyes, Plum. *The Debutante Divorcée*—for similar themes, setting, and humor.

Susan Kelly

The Last of Something

Susan Kelly grew up in Rutherford, North Carolina. She graduated from the University of North Carolina at Chapel Hill with a degree in English. She received her M.F.A. in fine arts and creative writing at the Program for Writers at Warren Wilson College. Her first novel, *How Close We Come*, was published when she won a contest at a small publishing house. The novel was subsequently bought outright by Warner Books. She and her husband Sterling have three grown children. The couple resides in Greensboro, North Carolina.

Plot Summary: Three college friends, Shotsie, Bess, and Claire, prepare Shotsie's mother's beach house for a weekend together while they wait for their husbands and the fourth member of their circle, Ian, to arrive. Each of the women has dated Ian in the past and each of them has an unhealthy obsession with him. Over the course of the weekend, marriages and friendships will be tested, and life-changing decisions will be made.

Publication Date: 2006

Number of Pages: 192

Geographic Setting: North Carolina

Time Period: Present day

Series Notes: This is a stand-alone novel.

Subject Headings: Female friendship—Fiction; Hurricanes—Fiction; North Carolina—Fiction

Appeal Points: Middle-aged women dealing with regret, multiple storylines.

DISCUSSION QUESTIONS

- Shotsie, Bess, and Claire all have regrets. What does each woman regret?
- What are the correlations between Ian and the storm?

- Do you think Shotsie's recent hysterectomy has anything to do with her sense of dissatisfaction? Do you think this is a normal side effect of that surgery?
- How does each weekend guest become injured either physically or mentally?
- What do you think the title *The Last of Something* means?

WEBSITE

http://susanskelly.com/

READERS' GUIDE

None available.

READ-ALIKES

Duncan, Pamela. *Plant Life*—for similar themes and setting.
Lunstrom, Kirsten Sundberg. *The Life She's Chosen: Stories*—for similar themes.
Stokes, Penelope. *Circle of Grace*—for similar themes and setting.

Cassandra King

The Same Sweet Girls

Cassandra King was born in Dothan, Alabama, on September 18, 1944. She is known for her novels featuring strong Southern women. Before turning her hand to fiction, King worked as a college writing professor and a reporter for an Alabama newspaper. King is married to the author Pat Conroy. They make their home in South Carolina.

Plot Summary: *The Same Sweet Girls* are anything but sweet. This is the story of six college friends who have met biannually for 30 years. They meet at Dauphin Island, where Lanier is mourning the loss of her marriage and custody of her children. There is Julia, the regal and contained first lady of Alabama, and Astor, a New York City dancer with a penchant for flirtation. Corrine is a gourd artist who has led a life of mental illness, poverty, and abuse. Each woman has a secret that she holds close even as they share food, laughter, and friendship. Devastating news brings them closer together, proving that it is during the toughest of times that you find out who your friends really are.

Publication Date: 2005

Number of Pages: 416

Geographic Setting: Alabama

Time Period: Present day.

Series Notes: This is a stand-alone novel.

Subject Headings: Women—Southern states—Fiction; Middle-aged women—Fiction; Female Friendship—Fiction; Southern states—Fiction

Appeal Points: Three-dimensional primary and secondary characters and graphic detail of scenery.

DISCUSSION QUESTIONS

- What is the role of Lanier's lesson book in the story? How do the other women learn from Lanier's lessons? If you had a lesson book, what is a lesson that would be in it?

- Early on, Corrine talks about the sweetness of Southern women. Does she believe they are really sweet? What do you think is more important, honesty or politeness? Do you believe that Southern manners are that different from those in other parts of the country?

- Discuss the men in these women's lives. Would you consider them good matches? What does the character of each man tell you about the woman he is involved with?

- Discuss how each of the women evolves over the course of the novel. Do all of them grow in a way that makes them somehow better than they were before?

- Discuss the importance of Bethany's blindness. How do Julia, Jo Ed, and Julia's mother react to her?

- What is the significance of Cal's relationship with Julia? With Corrine?

- Discuss Miles and Corrine's relationship. How did you feel when Corrine finally stood up for herself?

- Discuss Corrine's relationship with her son. Did you blame him for the way he treated his mother throughout the majority of the novel?

- Discuss Roseanelle. None of the girls really like her. Why does she stay on with the group?

- At the start of the novel, we learn that one of the original Same Sweet Girls passed away very young. How does that death overshadow the group and, eventually, Corrine's illness?

- Corrine asks her friends to help her die. Is this something you could ever do for a friend?

WEBSITE

http://www.cassandrakingconroy.com/

READERS' GUIDE

http://www.readinggroupguides.com/guides3/same_sweet_girls1.asp

READ-ALIKES

Berg, Elizabeth. *The Year of Pleasures: A Novel*—similar themes and writing style.

Brown, Jill Connor. *The Sweet Potato Queen's Book of Love*—similar tone and setting.

Diamant, Anita. *Good Harbor*—similar themes.

Barbara Kingsolver

Prodigal Summer

Barbara Kingsolver was born on April 8, 1955, in Annapolis, Maryland. She spent some time in Africa, where her father was a doctor. Most of her childhood was spent in Carlisle, Kentucky. She attended DePauw University, where she majored in biology. She studied ecology and evolutionary biology at the University of Arizona, where she earned her master's degree. Before becoming a writer, she worked as a housekeeper, a biological researcher, a copy editor, and an archeological digger. Kingsolver is the author of 13 works including fiction, nonfiction, essays, and short stories.

Her first novel, *The Bean Trees*, was published in 1988. Her work has earned her the National Book Prize of South Africa, has been shortlisted for a Pulitzer Prize and the PEN/Faulkner Award, and was chosen as an Oprah Book Choice. She was awarded the National Humanities Medal in 2000. In 1994, she was awarded an Honorary Doctorate of Letters from DePauw University. She received the same award from Duke University in 2008.

Along with authors Amy Tan, Matt Groening, Dave Barry, and Stephen King, she is in a band called The Rock Bottom Remainders. Kingsolver and her husband Emory live in Emory, Virginia, with their combined children.

Plot Summary: This is the story of three women in a small town in Southern Appalachia. Deana is a Forest Service wildlife biologist who spends most of the year up on the mountain, scaring off hunters and protecting a family of coyotes. Lusa, an entomologist from the city, struggles to fit in on the farm with her husband's family in the shadow of their mother. Nannie is an apple grower and conservationist who is at odds with her cranky old neighbor who periodically sprays her trees with DDT. Each woman faces challenges while trying to find a place where she fits in.

Publication Date: 2000

Number of Pages: 444

Geographic Setting: Southern Appalachia

Time Period: Present day

Series Notes: This is a stand-alone novel.

Subject Headings: Farm life—Fiction; Appalachian region, Southern—Fiction

Appeal Points: Literary writing, multiple plotlines, women's lives, detailed setting, and leisurely pace.

DISCUSSION QUESTIONS

- In what ways does Luna feel alienated in her new family? Why does she choose to stay?
- Why do you think Deana is saw drawn to the hunter?
- Garrett and Nannie are very different philosophically. Do you believe it is realistic for them to end up together?
- Describe the ways in which setting is a character in the novel.
- What do you think the title *Prodigal Summer* means?

WEBSITE

http://www.kingsolver.com/

READERS' GUIDE

http://www.readinggroupguides.com/guides_P/prodigal_summer1.asp
http://www.bookbrowse.com/reading_guides/detail/index.cfm?book_number=660

READ-ALIKES

Allende, Isabel. *The House of Spirits*—for similar themes and literary writing style.
Dillard, Annie. *The Living*—for similar themes and literary writing style.
McDermott, Alice. *After This*—for literary writing quality, strong female characters, and detailed setting.

Sophie Kinsella

Remember Me?

Sophie Kinsella is the pen name of Madeline Wickham. She was born Madeline Townley on December 12, 1969, in London, England. Kinsella was educated at New College, Oxford. Before turning her talents to fiction writing, she worked as a financial journalist. Kinsella is known for her breezy chick lit novels, in particular her *Shopaholic* series. She writes more serious women's fiction under her own name, Madeline Wickham. She and her husband Henry live in Hertfordshire, England, with their three sons. Mr. Wickham is the headmaster of a boy's preparatory school.

Plot Summary: Lexi Smart wakes up in a hospital bed in 2007. She is an accomplished businesswoman with a great loft apartment and a sexy husband. The only problem is, she thinks it is 2004 and that she's working in a dead-end job and has a loser boyfriend. While she is missing a huge chunk of her memory, she's thrilled to know that her life is not anywhere near as bad as she remembers it being. Then she discovers that she has no friends, that her coworkers despise her, and that she was about to leave her husband for another man.

Publication Date: 2008

Number of Pages: 384

Geographic Setting: London, England

Time Period: 2007

Series Notes: This is a stand-alone novel.

Subject Headings: Accident victims—Fiction; Amnesia—Fiction; Young women—Fiction

Appeal Points: Humor with a fast-paced style.

DISCUSSION QUESTIONS

- Think about your own life. Now think about the past three years of it being erased from your memory. What would you miss?

- What effect did the death of Lexi's father have on her? What effect did it have on her mother?
- What do you think becomes of Jon and Lexi after the book ends?
- If you were Lexi, would you give it all up for love?
- Have you read Kinsella's other novels? What does this one have in common with her other titles?

WEBSITE

http://www.randomhouse.com/bantamdell/kinsella/

READERS' GUIDE

http://www.readinggroupguides.com/guides_R/remember_me1.asp

READ-ALIKES

Fielding, Helen. *Bridget Jones's Diary*—for similar pacing, humor, and setting.

Keyes, Marian. *Lucy Sullivan Is Getting Married*—for similar pacing, humor, and setting.

Strohmeyer, Sarah. *Bubbles Unbound*—for similar pacing, humor, and strong female protagonist.

Lisa Kleypas

Smooth Talking Stranger

Lisa Kleypas was born in Texas in 1964. She attended Wellesley College in Massachusetts, where she studied political science. In 1984, she was named Miss Massachusetts and went on to compete in the Miss America pageant. She began writing fiction during her college breaks. Two months after graduation, she published her first novel, *Where Passion Leads*. While primarily known for her historical novels, she began writing contemporary romances in 2006.

Plot Summary: Advice columnist Ella Varner has a great job and a nice boyfriend. Her life is steady and predictable. Then her sister Tara leaves her newborn with Ella's mother, who calls and insists that Ella travel to Houston and take charge of the baby. When Ella arrives, her first order of business is talking with her sister's friends in the hope of discovering who the baby's father is. The likely candidate turns out to be millionaire Jack Travis, real estate developer and playboy extraordinaire. As Ella tries to convince Jack to step up to the plate, a mutual attraction develops between them. Ella also begins to have motherly feelings toward baby Luke, leaving her to wonder what will happen when and if her sister returns.

Publication Date: 2009

Number of Pages: 340

Geographic Setting: Texas

Time Period: Present day

Series Notes: This is a stand-alone novel.

Subject Headings: Millionaires—Texas—Fiction; Abandoned children—Fiction; Birth fathers—Fiction

Appeal Points: Character-driven, relaxed pacing, humorous, heart-warming, steamy

DISCUSSION QUESTIONS

- What events in Ella's life have helped form her into the woman she is at the beginning of the novel?
- Ella is placed in an impossible situation. Her mother tells her to come get baby Luke or she will put him in foster care. Her boyfriend tells her that if she comes home with a baby, he will be gone. What would you do in this situation?
- Given that Ella seems to be somewhat commitment phobic, why do you think she gives in to her attraction to Jack so quickly? Did you find this believable?
- Each of the main characters has her or his own baggage. What baggage does each character carry from the past?
- Discuss the mother/child bond in this novel. Does Tara feel it at all? When? Do you believe that a nonbiological mother can have the same kind of mother/child bond that a biological mother can experience?
- Did you figure out who the father of the baby was? When did you figure it out? What clues led you to your conclusion?

WEBSITE

http://www.lisakleypas.com/

READERS' GUIDE

None available.

READ-ALIKES

Child, Maureen. *Turn My World Upside Down*—for similar tone and pacing.
Phillips, Carly. *The Heartbreaker*—for similar tone and pacing.
Wolf, Joan. *High Meadow*—for similar themes.

Anne Lamott

Blue Shoe

Anne Lamott was born in San Francisco, California, on April 10, 1954. She is the daughter of author Kenneth Lamott. Lamott graduated from the Drew School in San Francisco (a preparatory high school). She is the author of both fiction and nonfiction. Her writing covers serious topics, such as motherhood, alcoholism, death, and spirituality. Her first novel, *Hard Laughter*, was published by Viking Press in 1980. Lamott's life is chronicled in a 1999 documentary by Frieda Lee Mock titled *Bird by Bird with Annie: A Film Portrait of the Writer Anne Lamott*. Lamott has one son, Sam. They reside in the San Francisco area.

Plot Summary: Recently divorced Mattie Ryder is raising her two children on her own in a rat-infested house. She has a strained relationship with her mother and questions about her deceased father. In addition, her mother is beginning to show signs of dementia, and her ex-husband has taken up with another woman. When she discovers a bag full of trinkets, secrets from the past come to the forefront, helping her to understand why her mother has been such a difficult woman for so long.

Publication Date: 2002

Number of Pages: 291

Geographic Setting: San Francisco, California

Time Period: Present

Series Notes: This is a stand-alone novel.

Subject Headings: Mothers and daughters—Fiction; Female friendship—Fiction; Divorced women—Fiction; Single mothers—Fiction; San Francisco (Calif.)—Fiction

Appeal Points: Even pacing, serious subjects, humor, and believable main and supporting characters.

DISCUSSION QUESTIONS

- How did Alfred's infidelities affect Isa? Mattie? What about Al?
- Even though Nicky has cheated on her, Mattie continues to sleep with him after she leaves him. Why do you think she does this? Is it lack of self-control? Is she trying to fill a need? What kind of need? Have you ever continued to be involved with someone you ended a relationship with? Why?
- While Mattie considers herself a woman of faith, she falls in love with a married man. Discuss the role that faith plays for each of the main characters in the novel.
- In what ways do the children react to their parent's divorce? How does Mattie try to counter the loss they feel?
- What do you think Lamott's definition of a family would be? What is your definition?

WEBSITE

http://www.barclayagency.com/lamott.html

READERS' GUIDE

http://us.penguingroup.com/static/rguides/us/blueshoe.html

READ-ALIKES

Berg, Elizabeth. *Open House*—for similar themes and tone.
McDermott, Alice. *Child of My Heart*—for similar tone and style.
Samuel, Barbara. *A Piece of Heaven*—for similar themes, tone, and religious undertones.

Lorna Landvik

Angry Housewives Eating Bon-Bons

Lorna Landvik was born on December 12, 1954, in Grand Forks, North Dakota, but lived most of her life in Minnesota. Before publishing fiction, Landvik worked as a chamber maid and English tutor in Bavaria. In California, she worked as an improvisational and stand-up comedian. She also worked at the Playboy mansion. Her debut novel, *Patty Jane's House of Curl*, was published in 1995. Landvik, her husband, and two children make their home in Minnesota.

Plot Summary: In 1968, Faith Owens, who has recently moved from Texas to Minnesota, is holed up in her house during a vicious snowstorm when she realizes that there are four crazy women having a snowball fight in her backyard. These women—Merit, Audrey, Slip, and Kari—are her neighbors. She becomes friends with the women, who decide to form a book group in order to get through the winter. The friends and their book club see each other through the next 30 years. They support each other through marriages and divorces, child rearing and cancer.

Publication Date: 2003

Number of Pages: 336

Geographic Setting: Minnesota

Time Period: 1968–1998

Series Notes: This is a stand-alone novel.

Subject Headings: Female friendship—Fiction; Housewives—Fiction; Book clubs (discussion groups)—Fiction; Minnesota—Fiction

Appeal Points: Humor, even pacing, and a well-drawn setting.

DISCUSSION QUESTIONS

- Several of the characters in the novel have secrets that they are trying to hide. What are they and how do they affect the way each character lives his/her life?

- The novel is narrated by each of the five women in turn. Did you like this device? What do you think it added or subtracted from the story?
- The novel is set in Minnesota. Did you find that the story had a Midwestern feel to it? Would it have been the same story had it been set elsewhere?
- Talk about the dynamics of the Freesia Court Book Group. Did you feel it was typical of book groups? Did the fact that each member lived on the same street add another layer to it? What types of book group experiences have you had?
- Though each woman has secrets or troubles, each also has strength. What is each woman's strength?
- Do you have friendships that have lasted over the years? In what ways have those friendships changed over time?

WEBSITE

http://www.randomhouse.com/features/lornalandvik/

READERS' GUIDE

http://www.randomhouse.com/rhpg/rc/library/display.pperl?isbn=97803454 42826&view=rg
http://www.readinggroupguides.com/guides3/angry_housewives_eating1.asp
http://www.bookmovement.com/app/readingguide/view.php?readingGuideID =1101

READ-ALIKES

Fowler, Karen Joy. *The Jane Austen Book Club*—for similar themes.
Monroe, Mary Alice. *The Book Club*—for similar themes and descriptions.
Noble, Elizabeth. *The Reading Group*—for similar themes and tone.

Erin McCarthy

Heiress for Hire

Erin McCarthy's first novel, *Bad Boys Online*, was published in 2003 after she won a contest for new writers on author Lori Foster's website. She has written 24 novels to date, including contemporary and paranormal romances. She writes paranormal young adult novels under the name Erin Lynn. McCarthy is married with two children and currently lives in Ohio.

Plot Summary: Amanda Delmar's rich daddy is tired of her spending habits. When she follows a friend to Ohio and calls asking him for more money, he decides he has had enough and cuts her off. Danny Tucker is a hardworking farmer who loves his parents and who has just discovered that he has an eight-year-old daughter he never knew about. His parents convince him to hire Erin as a nanny, which he does. Erin, for her part, does amazingly well, even though she's never had to lift a finger to help herself. Soon, the three are bonding, but their happiness may be short lived when the child's abusive stepfather reappears.

Publication Date: 2006

Number of Pages: 304

Geographic Setting: Ohio

Time Period: Present day

Series Notes: This is the second book in the Cuttserville, Ohio, series.

Subject Headings: Socialites—Fiction; Single women—Fiction; Single fathers—Fiction; Nannies—Fiction; Farmers—Fiction; Ohio—Fiction

Appeal Points: Contemporary romance, humor, and a quick read.

DISCUSSION QUESTIONS

- Do you believe that two people as different as Danny and Amanda can make a go of it?

- Discuss the relationship between Danny and his ex-wife Shelby. Why do you think they are able to stay friends following their divorce? In what ways does Shelby help both Danny and Amanda?
- Discuss Piper's relationship with each person in the novel. How does it vary from person to person? Does it make sense that she would have a more difficult time warming up to the men in the story?
- How does Amanda change over the course of the novel? What mitigates these changes?
- Many romance novels feature bad boys as heroes. Danny is an all-around nice guy. What was your reaction to him? What kind of man do you usually fall for?

WEBSITE

http://www.erinmccarthy.net/

READERS' GUIDE

None available.

READ-ALIKES

Crusie, Jennifer. *Crazy for You*—for similar setting, tone, and pacing.
Donovan, Susan. *The Girl Most Likely To*—for similar tone, pacing, and humor.
Gibson, Rachel. *Truly, Madly Yours*—for small-town setting, tone, humor, and pacing.

Debbie Macomber

Twenty Wishes

Debbie Macomber was born on October 22, 1948, in Yakima, Washington. She attended community college. Because she was dyslexic with four young children, friends and family tried to discourage her from a career in writing. Her perseverance paid off in 1984 with the publication of her first novel, *Heartsong*. Since that time, Macomber has become a national bestselling author with more than 80 titles and 13 series to her credit. Her work has appeared on *The New York Times* bestseller list. In 2008, Leisure Books introduced her line of Knitting Notions. All proceeds from the sale of those books will go to knitting charities and World Vision. Macomber is a three-time winner of the B. Dalton Award and has won a Lifetime Achievement Award from *Romantic Times* magazine. She and her husband Wayne still live in Washington State and winter in Florida.

Plot Summary: *Twenty Wishes* is part of Macomber's Blossom Street series. Thirty-eight-year-old Anne Marie Roche owns a bookstore on Seattle's Blossom Street and is recently widowed. Prior to his death, she and her husband had been separated over her desire to have a baby. She has a tenuous relationship with her husband's son and daughter from a previous marriage.

Anne Marie is joined on Valentine's Day by three other widows. Lillie and her daughter Barbie lost their husbands in the same plane crash; Elise's husband died of cancer. Each woman is feeling lonely and unfulfilled. They decide to each create a list of 20 wishes, things they have always wanted to do but never did. The novel unfolds as each of these women works towards her goals.

Publication Date: 2008

Number of Pages: 368

Geographic Setting: Seattle, Washington

Time Period: Present day

Series Notes: This is the fourth book in the Blossom Street series.

Subject Headings: Female friendship—Fiction; Booksellers and bookselling—Fiction; Loss (psychology)—Fiction; Pacific Northwest—Fiction

Appeal Points: Themes of loss and hope, with strong relationships between family members and friends.

DISCUSSION QUESTIONS

- Have you seen the movie *The Bucket List*? If so, compare that film with the novel.
- Do you believe that writing down your goals and wishes helps you to achieve them? Have you ever written such a list?
- Anne-Marie's relationship with Melissa is transformed throughout the novel. What do you think was the reason for the initial animosity between the two women? How has Robert's death brought them closer together?
- When Barbie meets Mark at the movie theater, he is very rude to her. He continues to be rude for quite some time. What makes him behave this way? Why is Barbie attracted to him?
- What do you think of the separation between Anne-Marie and Robert? Was she unreasonable in wanting children? Why? How do you think Robert would have reacted to the birth of his illegitimate child?
- Why is Lillie so attracted to Hector? Given their differences, do you think they can sustain a relationship over time?
- Anne-Marie is initially unsure of her involvement in the Lunch Buddy program. Why does she follow through with it?
- Discuss Anne-Marie and Ellen's relationship. How do they transform each other throughout the course of the novel?
- What would your list of 20 wishes look like?

WEBSITE

http://www.debbiemacomber.com/index.cfm

READERS' GUIDE

http://www.debbiemacomber.com/index.cfm?fuseaction=twenty_wishes
http://www.readinggroupchoices.com/search/details.cfm?id=761

READ-ALIKES

Berg, Elizabeth. *The Year of Pleasures*—for similar themes, characters, and tone.

Sutherland, Regina Hale. *The Red Hat Society's Acting Their Age*—for similar characters, themes, and tone.

Wiggs, Susan. *The Ocean Between Us*—for similar themes of marital unhappiness and self-discovery.

Susan Mallery

Under Her Skin

Susan Mallery is the pseudonym of Susan Macias. She is the author of more than 100 romance and women's fiction titles. Before earning her master's degree in creative writing, Susan worked as an accountant. Her first novel, *Tender Loving Care*, was published in 1991. She is the winner of numerous awards, including a *Romantic Times* Award for Best Silhouette Special edition. Mallery and her husband live in the Pacific Northwest.

Plot Summary: Silver-spooned Lexi Titan has built a successful day spa business without daddy's help. Now the bank is calling in her loan and she must come up with two million dollars in 30 days or lose everything. Cruz Rodriguez may be a successful businessman, but he lacks the social contacts that someone like Lizi can provide. He makes her an offer she can't refuse: tell everyone that they are engaged and move in with him for six months. During that time, she will introduce him to the members of high society. In exchange, he'll provide her with the money she needs to save her shop. Lexi and Cruz have a history together. Will they let it get in the way of their future?

Publication Date: 2009

Number of Pages: 328

Geographic Setting: Texas

Time Period: Present day

Series Notes: Lone Star Sisters, Book 1

Subject Headings: Women business owners; Sibling rivalry; Family businesses; Men–women relations; Texas—Fiction; Contemporary romances

Appeal Points: Well-developed characters, humor and emotion, and fast-paced plot.

DISCUSSION QUESTIONS

- Cruz witnessed his parents' abusive relationship. How does that affect his ability and desire to be in a serious relationship himself?

- Why doesn't Lexi go to her father for the money she needs to pay off her loan?
- Cruz gives Lexi the money she needs in exchange for the connections she can provide him with. Do you have a problem with this kind of exchange? Why or why not?
- Discuss Cruz's relationship with his daughter.
- What are the similarities and differences between Cruz and Lexi's fathers?

WEBSITE

http://www.susanmallery.com/

READERS' GUIDE

No guide available.

READ-ALIKES

Child, Maureen. *A Crazy Kind of Love*—for similar themes and pacing.
Donahue, Tina. *Close to Perfect*—for similar themes, humor, and pacing.
Macomber, Debbie. *The Playboy and the Widow*—for similar themes and writing.

Jo-Ann Mapson

Bad Girl Creek

Jo-Ann Mapson received her M.F.A. from Vermont College. She has worked as a writer, poet, and teacher. Her first novel, *Fault Line*, was published in 1990. Mapson currently resides in Costa Mesa, California.

Plot Summary: Wheelchair-bound Phoebe DeThomas has just inherited a flower farm on the coast of California from her favorite Aunt Sadie. Her brother James would love to get his hands on it—that, or force her to sell it so that she would have something to live on. Phoebe, however, has other plans. Wanting to be self-sufficient but knowing that she can't make a go of the farm on her own, she places an ad in the local newspaper for free room and board in exchange for work on the farm. Nance, who has lost her job and fears she might have AIDS, is the first to answer the advertisement. Before long, Nance and Beryl join them. Each of the women is struggling to overcome her own issues. As friendships form and the women become family, they forge ahead to turn the farm profitable. This is a tender story of women who rely on each other to overcome obstacles.

Publication Date: 2001

Number of Pages: 381

Geographic Setting: California

Time Period: Present day

Series Notes: This is the first book in the Bad Girl Creek trilogy.

Subject Headings: Women gardeners—Fiction; Women with disabilities—Fiction; Female friendship—Fiction; Floriculturists—Fiction; California—Fiction; California—Fiction

Appeal Points: Strong female characters overcoming adversity through friendship, a character-driven plot, even pace, and humor.

DISCUSSION QUESTIONS

- Many people (both men and women) in Phoebe's place would have given in to James's push to sell the farm and be taken care of for life.

What it is about Phoebe and her past that lead her to make the decision she makes?

- Discuss each of the main characters. What obstacle does each one have to overcome? What are the ways in which they change over the course of the novel?
- What role do pets play in the novel? Discuss each woman's relationship with her pet.
- Discuss Phoebe's relationship with her brother. In what ways does James change over the course of the novel?
- Discuss the idea of family as it is presented in the novel. What is your own definition of family?
- Think about your own friends. In what ways have you supported each other in the past?

WEBSITE

http://web.me.com/jamapson/Site_3/Welcome.html

READERS' GUIDE

None available.

READ-ALIKES

Ball, Donna. *A Year on Ladybug Farm*—for similar themes of life-changing events, female friendship, and overcoming obstacles.

Bauermeister, Erica. *The School of Essential Ingredients*—for similar themes of self-perception, self-discovery, and female friendship.

Stockett, Kathryn. *The Help*—for similar themes of women's friendships and empowerment.

Wendy Markham

That's Amore

Wendy Markham is the pseudonym for Wendy Corsi Staub. She is best known for her single-title psychological suspense novels, which she publishes under her own name. She publishes women's fiction under the name Wendy Markham. Her works under both names have been translated into more than a dozen languages.

Wendy was raised in New York State. She worked in independent bookstores during college and moved to New York City at the age of 21 to pursue a career in writing. She worked as a book editor and an account manager for an advertising agency before publishing her first novel, *Summer Lightning*. She now lives in the suburbs of New York with her husband and two children.

Plot Summary: Ralphie Chickalini is still mourning the death of his father. He thinks that may be why he is suddenly getting cold feet when it comes to his fiancée, Francesca Maria Buccigrossi. Everyone in the Chickalini clan loves Francesca and his father had dubbed her a keeper. Why, then, is he relieved on New Year's Eve when she announces that she does not want to marry him? Is he suddenly happy? And why can't he keep his mind off of the woman he just met at the bar?

Daria is in town visiting her sister while she tries to figure out where she belongs. Like her parents, Daria has always been a wanderer, living in various places and never staying for very long. Even her brief stint at marriage was a failure. When she meets Ralph Chickalini and his family after leaving her phone behind at the family's pizza parlor, she admits she's attracted. That doesn't mean, however, that she should give in to her longing for him or her desire to have a family and roots, but that's exactly where she's headed, especially if the deceased elder Chickalini has anything to do with it.

Publication Date: 2008

Number of Pages: 352

Geographic Setting: Queens, New York

Time Period: Present day

Series Notes: This is a stand-alone novel.

Subject Headings: Psychics—Fiction; Sisters—Fiction; Contemporary romances; Love stories—American

Appeal Points: This is a sweet, quick read with lots of humor and endearing characters. Fans of paranormal romances will enjoy the catalyst for Ralphie and Daria's growth as individuals.

DISCUSSION QUESTIONS

- Daria and her sister Tammy both have psychic abilities. Tammy embraces hers. Why has Daria turned her back on hers?
- We are told that the entire Chickalini family adored Maria. Mr. Chickalini even told Ralphie that she was a keeper. Why, then, are Ralphie's sisters, brothers-in-law, and even their children so welcoming to Daria? Why is Mr. Chickalini reaching out from the grave to bring the two of them together?
- Daria says that her first failed marriage was an attempt to have the kind of family and sense of belonging that she has always searched for. How is her eventual marriage to Ralphie any different?
- Was Daria right in not telling Ralphie that she decided to stay in New York? What was the result of that decision? Was it a positive one?
- Do you come from a large family? If so, how does the Chickalini family compare with yours? If not, have you ever longed for a large family?
- Daria thinks the Chickalini family, with all of their nosiness and compassion, are wonderful. Ralphie loves them, too, but he sees the downside to a large family as well. What about a large family might be bothersome?
- Do you feel we learn enough about Maria in the novel? Why does she decide not to marry Ralphie? Do you believe she moves on too fast? What about Ralphie?

WEBSITE

http://www.wendycorsistaub.com/index.html

READERS' GUIDE

None available.

READ-ALIKES

Donovan, Susan—*Take a Chance on Me*—for similar pacing and tone.
Grayson, Kristine. *Simply Irresistible*—for similar writing style and tone.
Phillips, Susan Elizabeth—*It Had To Be You*—for similar themes, pacing, and tone.

Carole Matthews

The Chocolate Lovers' Club

Carole Matthews was born in St. Helens, Merseyside, England. She studied beauty therapy at Champneys College. Before turning to novels, Matthews worked as a secretary, beauty therapist, television presenter, and freelance writer. Her first novel, *Let's Meet on Platform Eight*, was published in 1997. It was adapted to film and released under the name *A Compromising Position*. Matthews currently resides in Milton Keynes, England.

Plot Summary: The Chocolate Lovers' Club is composed of a group of four women who get together at a high-end chocolatier to hash out problems, plan revenge on cheating boyfriends, and complain about their spouses. Lucy Lombard is as addicted to her wandering boyfriend as she is chocolate. Nadia's husband is gambling away all of their savings. Autumn's drug-addict brother has just moved in with her, and Chantel has been cheating on her husband—with a man who just took off with all of her jewels. Through thick and thin, one wacky adventure at a time, the women are there for each other, providing a shoulder to cry on and a box of chocolates to soothe the weary soul.

Publication Date: 2008

Number of Pages: 320

Geographic Setting: London

Time Period: Present day.

Series Notes: This is a stand-alone novel.

Subject Headings: Female friendship—Fiction; Chocolate—Fiction; Chocolatiers—Fiction; London (England)—Fiction

Appeal Points: Chick lit with lots of humor and steady pacing.

DISCUSSION QUESTIONS

- Why do you believe Lucy keeps forgiving her boyfriend for cheating? What would you be able to forgive or not to forgive in a partner?

- If Chantel is so unhappy in her marriage, why doesn't she leave?
- Chocolate is the medicine of choice for these women's emotional ups and downs. What do you comfort yourself with? What do you celebrate with?
- Which woman could you most relate to? Why?
- Discuss the men in the novel. Did you find them too one dimensional?
- Many of the characters suffer from addiction. Who are they and what are they addicted to?
- Have you ever been involved with someone who had an addiction? What was that like for you?

WEBSITE

http://www.carolematthews.com/

READERS' GUIDE

None available.

READ-ALIKES

Bagshawe, Lois. *The Go-to Girl*—for similar themes, tone, and style.

Harbison, Beth. *Shoe Addicts Anonymous*—for similar themes, tone, and style.

Markham, Wendy. *Never on a Sunday*—for similar themes, tone, and style.

Fern Michaels

The Scoop

Fern Michaels is the pseudonym of Mary Ruth Kuczkir. She grew up in Hastings, Pennsylvania. When she married, she moved to New Jersey. She was a stay-at-home mother until her youngest went to kindergarten. At that point, her husband insisted she get a job. Not having any marketable skills, she turned to writing. The couple subsequently divorced. She is now the author of 99 novels, many on *The New York Times* bestseller list. In 1993, she purchased a 300-year-old plantation house in South Carolina, which she remodeled and in which she now resides with the ghost of a woman called Mary Margaret. Michaels has been inducted into the New Jersey Literary Hall of Fame.

Plot Summary: Toots Loudenberry is a multimillionaire. She got that way by burying husbands. She has no sooner buried the eighth than she is off on a new adventure. Her journalist daughter is about to lose her job if the trashy newspaper she works for goes under. Toots has the means to save the paper and plans to do just that. With the aid of her septuagenarian friends Sophie, Mavis, and Ida, she jets off to Hollywood under the guise of a motherly visit. Things with the takeover don't go according to plan when the newspaper's publisher, Rodwell Archibald Godfrey III, takes off with the loot. What ensues is a hilarious chase to the Cayman Islands as the women try to catch Rodwell without having Toots's daughter catch on to their hijinks.

Publication Date: 2009

Number of Pages: 279

Geographic Setting: Charleston, South Carolina

Time Period: Present day

Series Notes: This is the first novel in the Godmothers series.

Subject Headings: Older women—Fiction; Female friendship—Fiction; Mothers and daughters—Fiction; Hollywood (Los Angeles, California)—Fiction

Appeal Points: Female friendship, humor, and hijinks with a touch of danger.

DISCUSSION QUESTIONS

- Toots, Sophie, and Ida may complain about a variety of things, but they are spunky older women. What kind of a woman do you hope to be when you get older?
- Not a week has passed when Toots takes off on her adventure. Do you think enough time has passed since her husband died? Does her immediate rebound say anything about her relationship with her husband or about how she feels about men in general?
- Sophie, Mavis, and Ida follow Toots on her wild goose chase. What is the craziest thing you have ever done for a friend?
- Discuss Toots' relationship with Abby.
- Discuss each of the main characters. Who was your favorite? Why?

WEBSITE

http://fernmichaels.com/

READERS' GUIDE

None available.

READ-ALIKES

Cohen, Paula Marantz. *Jane Austen in Boca*—for similar characters, humor, and pacing.
Dalby, Rob. *Waltzing at the Piggly Wiggly*—for similar characters, humor, and pacing.
Ross, Ann B. *Miss Julia Speaks Her Mind*—for similar characters, humor, and pacing.

Sue Miller

The World Below

Sue Miller was born in 1943. She received her bachelor's degree from Radcliffe College in 1964. She has worked as a day-care provider, a high school teacher, a waitress, a model, and a researcher. She was the recipient of the Pushcart Award in 1984.

Miller did not begin writing until she was 35 years old, when she published her first novel, *The Good Mother*, in 1986. The success of that novel was recognized by Hollywood and made into a movie featuring Diane Keaton and Liam Neeson in 1988.

Miller is married to fellow writer Doug Bauer and lives in Boston, Massachusetts. She has one child from her first marriage.

Plot Summary: Fifty-two-year-old Catherine Hubbard leaves San Francisco and travels to Vermont when she learns that she and her brother have inherited their grandparents' home. While there, she discovers her grandmother's old diaries in the attic and begins a journey to understand the woman she thought she knew. Along the way, she must come to terms with her own two divorces and her relationship with her mother and learn to trust in love again.

Publication Date: 2001

Number of Pages: 275

Geographic Setting: Vermont

Time Period: 1919 and present day

Series Notes: This is a stand-alone novel.

Subject Headings: Inheritance and succession—Fiction; Home ownership—Fiction; Grandmothers—Fiction; Divorced people—Fiction; Vermont—Fiction

Appeal Points: Literary writing, family relationships, and the effect of the past on the present. Much of the novel is told in journal format and covers two different time periods. Strong sense of place.

DISCUSSION QUESTIONS

- Discuss the similarities between Georgia and Catherine.
- Dr. Holbrook feels that he is saving Georgia. Does she need saving?
- In what ways does Georgia show her independence?
- Discuss the relevance of the title.
- Discuss the idea of love in the novel.
- In what ways do the characters in the novel escape their reality?

WEBSITE

This author does not have an official website.

READERS' GUIDE

http://www.randomhouse.com/catalog/display.pperl?isbn=9780345440761
&view=rg

READ-ALIKES

Bauer, Ann. *A Wild Ride Up the Cupboards*—for similar tone and themes.

Paddock, Jennifer. *A Secret World: A Novel*—for similar themes and style.

Wolitzer, Hilma. *The Doctor's Daughter*—for similar writing style, tone, and themes.

Jacquelyn Mitchard

Twelve Times Blessed

Jacquelyn Mitchard was born on December 10, 1953. She attended Rockford College in Illinois. She received her B.A. in English in 1973. After graduation, she worked for a year as a teacher before returning home to Chicago to care for her ailing mother. She studied creative writing at the University of Illinois at Urbana–Champaign. She worked for *Pioneer Press*, *Capital Times*, and then the *Milwaukee Journal*. She married Dan Allegretti, a fellow journalist, in 1981 and began her family through both natural means and adoption. In 1993, Allegretti died of colon cancer.

Mitchard's first novel, *The Deep End of the Ocean*, sold to Viking Press in 1994. They also gave her a second book contract for $500,000. Mitchard now has three young adult novels, three children's books, and nine adult works of fiction to her credit. *The Deep End of the Ocean* was made into a movie featuring Michelle Pfeiffer, Treat Williams, and Whoopi Goldberg.

Mitchard and her husband, Chris Brent, live on Stony Hill in South Central Wisconsin. The couple have seven children.

Plot Summary: Widow True Dickinson runs a successful mail-order baby gift business on Cape Cod. She is a successful mother to a 10-year-old boy named Guy and has a terrific assistant and a myriad of friends. Still, she feels like something is missing from her life. A car accident introduces her to restaurateur Hank Bannister, who is 10 years her junior. Following a whirlwind romance, they marry. Frustrations abound as Hank tries to win over Guy. True's mother disapproves of her marriage, which puts a wrench in their relationship. Then True becomes pregnant, and Hank starts to feel the pressure.

Publication Date: 2003

Number of Pages: 544

Geographic Setting: Cape Cod, Massachusetts

Time Period: Present day

Series Notes: This is a stand-alone novel.

Subject Headings: Widows—Fiction; Single mothers—Fiction; Middle-aged women—Fiction; Young men—Fiction; Cape Cod (Massachusetts)—Fiction

Appeal Points: Lyrical writing, slow pacing, and in-depth characters.

DISCUSSION QUESTIONS

- Hank is clearly in love with True, but she is very insecure due to their age differences. Have you ever dated someone much younger than you? Do you think Hank would have felt insecure if he were the older of the two?
- Mitchard names her main character True Dickinson. Do you think this is a coincidence? Are there any similarities between True and Emily Dickinson?
- Do you believe in love at first sight?
- True's friends Isabelle, Franny, and Rudy are very important in her life. Who are Hank's friends? Do you think women's friendships differ from men's friendships? How?
- Do you believe in fate? If so, do you believe that people can change their fate?

WEBSITE

http://jackiemitchard.com/

READERS' GUIDE

http://www.readinggroupguides.com/guides3/12_times_blessed1.asp
http://www.harpercollins.com/author/authorExtra.aspx?authorID=2084
&isbn13=9780061032479&displayType=readingGuide

READ-ALIKES

Adler, Elizabeth. *The Last Time I Saw* Paris—for similar writing style and themes.
Berg, Elizabeth. *The Year of Pleasures*—for similar writing style and tone.
Spencer, LaVyrle. *Family Blessings*—for similar themes.

Laura Moriarty

While I'm Falling

Laura Moriarty was born in Honolulu, Hawaii, on December 4, 1979. She received her B.A. in social work and then went on to earn an M.A. in creative writing from the University of Kansas. She was the recipient of the George Bennett Fellowship for Creative Writing at Phillips Exeter Academy in New Hampshire. She currently lives with her daughter in Lawrence, Kansas.

Plot Summary: Veronica's parents' divorce after her father comes home early from a business trip to find the roofer asleep in his bed. Her father moves into a furnished condominium while her mother is forced to sell the house and move into a spare apartment. When she is evicted because she refuses to get rid of her aging dog, she sleeps at first in her car until the cold weather forces her to turn to Veronica, who is a resident assistant at college during her junior year.

Publication Date: 2009

Number of Pages: 352

Geographic Setting: Kansas

Time Period: Present day

Series Notes: This is a stand-alone novel.

Subject Headings: Mothers and daughters—Fiction; Divorce—Fiction; Women college students—Fiction, Domestic fiction

Appeal Points: Overcoming obstacles, strength in women, mother–daughter relationships, steady pacing.

DISCUSSION QUESTIONS

- From almost the beginning of the story, Natalie's idyllic life begins to crumble. What events led up to the indiscretion with the roofer?

- Why has Veronica chosen to pursue premed? What events cause her to consider changing her major to literature? Do you see this change as a success or a failure?
- Describe Veronica's relationship with her sister Elise.
- Do you believe Natalie had sex with the roofer? Does it matter?
- What caused Natalie's unhappiness with her marriage? Was her affair justified?
- Are there similarities between Natalie's affair with the roofer and Veronica's fling with Clyde?
- Do Veronica and Elise take sides in the divorce?

WEBSITE

http://www.lauramoriarty.net/

READERS' GUIDE

http://www.midwestbooksellers.org/site/wp-content/uploads/2009/07/whileimfallingrgg.pdf

READ-ALIKES

Austin, Lynn N. *All She Ever Wanted*—for similar themes.
Hood, Ann. *The Knitting Circle*—for similar writing style.
Yates, Richard. *The Easter Parade: A Novel*—for similar themes.

Sinead Moriarty

The Baby Trail

Sinead Moriarty was born and raised in Dublin. Her mother was a children's book author. Following college, Moriarty lived in both Paris and London. She currently lives in Dublin with her husband, two sons, and daughter.

Plot Summary: Emma Hamilton is a makeup artist whose biological clock is ticking. When she announces to her husband James that they should start a family, he is surprised but agrees. At first, they try the romantic approach. When that doesn't work, she turns to an infertility specialist. The couple's love life heads south as spontaneity is replaced with hormone treatments, unrelenting tests, and an in-vitro fertilization procedure.

Publication Date: 2005

Number of Pages: 320

Geographic Setting: Ireland

Time Period: Present day

Series Notes: This is the first book in the Emma and James series.

Subject Headings: Fertility, human—Fiction; Conception—Fiction; Ireland—Fiction; Chick lit

Appeal Points: Fast pace, emotion, and humor.

DISCUSSION QUESTIONS

- Despite the fact that her life is going well, Emma wants to have a baby desperately. Do you believe there is such a thing as a biological clock? Why does Emma feel she needs a baby in order to feel complete?
- Why does Emma finally decide to stop treatments?
- Do you feel that James was supportive enough of Emma?

- Emma's friend Jess is not happy that she is pregnant for the second time. Emma counters that she is the worse off of the two, because she wants a baby and can't have one. Who do you agree with?
- If you were having difficulty getting pregnant, do you think it would be difficult being around pregnant friends? Do you think Emma's reaction is realistic?
- Emma wants to adopt, but James is not so sure. What arguments does he present? Are his concerns realistic? Do you believe Emma gives enough thought to his concerns?

WEBSITE

http://www.sineadmoriarty.com/

READERS' GUIDE

http://www.readinggroupguides.com/guides3/baby_trail1.asp

READ-ALIKES

Berg, Elizabeth. *Until the Real Thing Comes Along*—for similar themes.
Moriarty, Sinead. *From Here to Maternity*—for similar themes.
Wiggs, Susan. *Just Breathe*—for similar themes.

Elizabeth Noble

Things I Want My Daughters to Know

Elizabeth Noble was born in England in December 1968. She grew up in both England and Canada. She received her B.A. in English and literature from Oxford University. Before becoming a full-time writer, she worked in the publishing industry. Her first novel, *The Reading Group*, was published in the UK in 2004 and immediately became a number-one best seller. She currently has four novels to her credit. Noble resides in New York City with her husband and their two daughters.

Plot Summary: Barbara has four grown daughters. Each of them, in her own way, has much growing up yet to do. Lisa is unable to make a commitment. Jennifer's marriage soured long ago and she has made no move to change its tired old patterns. Amanda has very little to do with the rest of her family. Teenage Hannah just might need the most guidance of them all. When Barbara discovers that she is dying of cancer, she decides to write a letter to each of her daughters in the hope that her words of wisdom will help them move through life without her. In the year following their mother's death, the girls struggle to overcome their loss and learn from the lessons she left them.

Publication Date: 2008

Number of Pages: 374

Geographic Setting: England

Time Period: Present day

Series Notes: This is a stand-alone novel.

Subject Headings: Sisters—Fiction; Mothers and daughters—Fiction

Appeal Points: Tearjerker, even pace, and well-developed characters.

DISCUSSION QUESTIONS

- Noble begins the novel after Barbara has already died. In what ways might the story have been different had the author started while the girls still had their mother with them?

- Each of the women in the novel is participating in escapist behavior. How does each of them escape dealing with the realities of life?
- The novel is told from multiple perspectives. How did this affect your reading of the novel and understanding of the characters?
- What piece of wisdom that Barbara left behind do you find most helpful?
- What role does Mark play in helping the girls get past their grief?

WEBSITE

http://www.elizabethnoblebooks.com/content/index.asp

READERS' GUIDE

http://www.readinggroupguides.com/guides_t/things_i_want_my_daughters
_to_know1.asp

READ-ALIKES

De los Santos, Marisa. *Belong to Me*—for an emotional read and well-developed characters.

Moriarty, Laura. *The Rest of Her Life: A Novel*—for an emotional read and well-developed characters.

Sparks, Nicholas. *Message in a Bottle*—for an emotional read and well-developed characters.

Tawni O'Dell

Sister Mine: A Novel

Tawni O'Dell was born in Indiana in 1964 and raised in Pennsylvania. She received her B.A. from Northwest University with a degree in journalism. She spent many years living and writing in Chicago before returning home to Pennsylvania, where she now resides with her husband Bernard Cohen and their two children. O'Dell is a *New York Times* bestselling author. Her novels have been translated into 10 languages and published in 20 countries.

Plot Summary: Shae-Lynn Penrose did not have an ideal childhood. Her mother died giving birth to her sister Shannon, who died at the hands of their abusive father while Shae-Lynn was away at college, but Shae-Lynn is a fighter. She gave birth to her son Clay out of wedlock when she herself was only a teen and has raised him on her own. She has put herself through college and worked as a policewoman. Now she is living back in her hometown, working as a cab driver, and her sister Shannon has mysteriously appeared, very much alive and pregnant with her 10th child.

Publication Date: 2007

Number of Pages: 405

Geographic Setting: Jolly Mount, Pennsylvania

Time Period: Present day

Series Notes: This is a stand-alone novel.

Subject Headings: Taxicab drivers—Fiction; Sisters—Fiction; Coal miners and mining—Fiction; Pennsylvania—Fiction

Appeal Points: Dark humor, family saga, with a character and plot-driven storyline.

DISCUSSION QUESTIONS

- Shae-Lynn becomes aware of the fact that her father was not the only abusive man in Jolly Mount. To what extent to you think coal mining plays a part in this situation?

- Why do you think that the Penroses' neighbors never stepped in to remove the girls from the home?
- Given Shae-Lynn's past, she has managed to raise Clay to become a responsible man. How do you think she managed this? What factors played a role in Clay's upbringing as opposed to his mother's?
- Describe Shae-Lynn's relationship with E. J. What do you think happens to them when the novel ends? Why?
- Compare and contrast Shae-Lynn and Shannon. Why do you think the two chose such different paths?
- Discuss O'Dell's use of black humor throughout the novel.
- Discuss the Jolly Mount Five. Do you think they made the right decision to drop their case against the owner of the mine? Why or why not?
- Do you believe that the cycle of abuse can ever be overcome? Are abused children destined to become abusive parents?

WEBSITE

http://www.tawniodell.com

READERS' GUIDE

http://www.litlovers.com/guide_coal_run.html

READ-ALIKES

Berg, Elizabeth. *What We Keep*—for similar themes.
McMurtry, Larry. *Terms of Endearment*—for dysfunctional families and similar tone.
Palmer, Liza. *A Field Guide to Burying Your Parents*—for dysfunctional families and similar tone.

Ann Packer

The Dive from Clausen's Pier

Ann Packer was born in 1959, the daughter of two educators. Her father taught law at Stanford University and her mother taught creative writing. Packer attended Yale University and later married Jon James, an architect. They have two children. Her first published work was a book of short stories, *Mendocino and Other Stories*, in 1994. Her first novel, *The Dive from Clausen's Pier*, was published in 2002.

Plot Summary: Twenty-three-year-old Carrie Bell has lived in Madison all of her life. She has dated Mike since they were in high school, and they are engaged to be married. The only problem is that she has fallen out of love with him. On Memorial Day, the couple take their annual drive to join their friends for a picnic. The tension between the two is thick. Carrie has just about made up her mind to leave Mike when he dives off of the pier into shallow water and ends up paralyzed. Now Carrie must decide whether to stay by the man who has been such a large part of her life or to move on as she originally planned and start a life different from the one she has always known.

Publication Date: 2002

Number of Pages: 369

Geographic Setting: Wisconsin

Time Period: Present day

Series Notes: This is a stand-alone novel.

Subject Headings: Young women—Fiction; Accident victims—Fiction; Wisconsin—Fiction

Appeal Points: Coming-of-age story, domestic fiction, theme driven, sparse prose, and witty dialogue.

DISCUSSION QUESTIONS

- Carrie and Mike became sweethearts in high school. Do you believe such a relationship can withstand the test of time? Why or why not?

- Carrie ultimately makes the decision to leave Madison and Mike to make a life for herself. Do you agree with her decision? Why or why not? What do you think you would have done in her situation?
- Discuss Kilroy. Why do you think Carrie is attracted to him? In what ways is he different from Mike? Are there any similarities between the two men?
- Were you surprised by Carrie's return home? How did the ending of the novel sit with you?
- To what extent do you believe we are indebted to those we love and who love us?
- To what extend do you believe our past and upbringing defines who we become as adults?

WEBSITE

http://www.annpacker.com

READERS' GUIDE

http://www.readinggroupguides.com/guides3/dive_from_clausens_pier1.asp

READ-ALIKES

Banks, Melissa. *The Wonder Spot*—for similar themes, tone, and pacing.
Moriarty, Laura. *The Rest of Her Life*—for similar themes and tone.
Picoult, Jodi. *My Sister's Keeper*—for similar themes and tone.

Carly Phillips

Hot Number

Carly Phillips was raised in Spring Valley, New York, where she attended Ramapo Senior High School. She met her husband Paul while attending Brandeis University. Upon finishing Brandeis, she enrolled in Boston University's School of Law. She passed both the Connecticut and New York bar exams. Phillips and her husband have two daughters. They currently reside in New York.

Plot Summary: Micki Jordan is a sports star publicist with the hots for Damian Fuller. Damien is a professional baseball player for the New York Renegades with a thing for the ladies. Too bad Micki is more tomboy than seductress. In order to woo Damian, Micki undergoes a makeover with results that get her more than she bargained for.

Publication Date: 2005

Number of Pages: 378

Geographic Setting: New York City

Time Period: Present day

Series Notes: This is the second title in Phillips' *Hot Zone* series.

Subject Headings: Women public relations personnel—Fiction; Athletes—Fiction; Man-woman relationships—Fiction; Single women—Fiction

Appeal Points: Sexual tension, humor, engaging characters, and a fast read.

DISCUSSION QUESTIONS

- Micki's transformation begins with a makeover. Have you ever tried to change your appearance to attract someone? How far would you be willing to go to transform yourself?
- Micki is the youngest of three girls. Does her position in the birth order affect her role in the family? Where are you in the birth order in your family? Do you believe position plays a part in your role in the family?

- Discuss Damian. Fame has given him everything. Is there a downside to his fame?
- How do Micki and her sisters try to help their uncle accept his physical disabilities?
- How does Damian convince Micki that he deserves her?

WEBSITE

http://www.carlyphillips.com

READERS' GUIDE

http://www.readinggroupguides.com/guides3/hot_number1.asp

READ-ALIKES

Markahm, Wendy. *Slightly Single*—for similar themes and tone.
White, Pat. *Ring Around My Heart*—for similar themes and tone.
Winters, Jill. *Blushing Pink*—for similar themes and tone.

Lily Prior

La Cucina: A Novel of Rapture

Lily Prior is a great lover of all things Italian and has traveled extensively in Sicily, where she developed the inspiration for *La Cucina*, her debut novel. She divides her time between London and Italy.

Plot Summary: Rosa Fiore has always found comfort in her mother's kitchen. As a teenager, the only thing she loved more than cooking was Bartholomew. When their affair ends, she turns first to her kitchen and then to librarianship. As a librarian in Palermo, she spends her evenings creating fabulous dishes and resigns herself to a life of solitude until she meets l'Inglese, who shares not only her bed but also her love of cooking.

Publication Date: 2000

Number of Pages: 263

Geographic Setting: Sicily, Italy

Time Period: Early 1900s

Series Notes: This is a stand-alone novel.

Subject Headings: Middle-aged women—Fiction; Women librarians—Fiction; Women cooks—Fiction; Cooking—Fiction; Sicily (Italy)—Fiction

Appeal Points: Sensuality, even pace, with descriptive writing.

DISCUSSION QUESTIONS

- In what way is food synonymous with sex in the novel? Is the sensuality of food particular to Italy? Do you think this novel would have been as effective had it been set elsewhere?
- Is the character of Rosa a cliché? Why or why not?
- Did you feel that Prior included too many details in the novel? Give an example.

- Did the division of the book into seasons throw you off in any way? Why do you suppose the author chose to set the book up in this way?
- How does Rosa's sense of identity change over the course of the novel?
- Who was your favorite member of Rosa's family and why?

WEBSITE

http://www.lilyprior.com

READERS' GUIDE

http://www.bookbrowse.com/reading_guides/detail/index.cfm/book_number/720/La-Cucina

READ-ALIKES

Allen, Sarah Addison. *Garden Spells*—for similar themes, writing style, and tone.

Esquival, Laura. *Like Water for Chocolate*—for similar themes, writing style, and tone.

Harris, Joanne. *Chocolat*—for similar themes, writing style, and tone.

Amanda Quick

The Perfect Poison

Amanda Quick is the pen name of author Jayne Ann Krentz. Under the name Amanda Quick, Krentz writes historical romantic suspense.

Krentz earned her B.A. in history from the University of California at Santa Cruz. She received her master's in library science from San Jose State University in San Jose, California. Before becoming a full-time writer, she worked as both an academic and corporate librarian. She and her husband Frank currently reside in Seattle, Washington.

Plot Summary: Lucinda Bromly, a member of the Arcane Society, possesses the ability to sense poison. Her talent has found her helping the police in murder investigations on more than one occasion. Now a wealthy lord has been murdered, and one of Lucinda's unique plants has been implicated in the murder. In order to hunt down the real killer and get the suspicion firmly away from her, she hires fellow Arcane Society member Caleb Jones, who finds himself as fascinated by Lucinda as he is by the case.

Publication Date: 2009

Number of Pages: 340

Geographic Setting: London, England

Time Period: Victorian Era

Series Notes: This is number six in the Arcane Society series.

Subject Headings: Women botanists—England—Fiction; Secret societies—England—Fiction; Psychic ability—Fiction; Murder investigations—Fiction

Appeal Points: Character-driven storyline, fast pace, suspense, witty dialogue, steaminess, historical romance.

DISCUSSION QUESTIONS

- Lucinda knows what has poisoned the victim but does not notify the police for fear they will accuse her. Did she make the right decision in not giving them that information? Why or why not?

- Even though Caleb is attracted to Lucinda, he has decided that he will never marry because he knows that insanity runs in his family. What would you do in a similar situation? What if it had been a physical disease rather than a mental one? Do you think that would have made a difference?

- How does Lucinda deal with the rumors that she murdered her fiancé? Do you find her reaction authentic?

- Have you read any of the other Arcane Society novels? Does this novel follow the same pattern? How is it similar? In what ways is it different?

- Caleb's family has been taking medicine to help their psychic abilities over the generations, and generations of his family have gone mad. What if there was a medicine today that could enhance one of your abilities? Would you take it? Why or why not? Compare Caleb's family's use of this medicine with the use of steroids in sports today.

WEBSITE

http://www.amandaquick.com

READERS' GUIDE

None available.

READ-ALIKES

Beverly, Jo. *An Arranged Marriage*—for character-driven storyline and similar tone.

Coulter, Catherine. *The Sherbrook Twins*—for character-driven storyline and similar tone.

Garlock, Dorothy. *Mother Road*—for character-driven and suspenseful storyline.

Kris Radish

Annie Freeman's Fabulous Traveling Funeral

Kris Radish was born in Milwaukee, Wisconsin, on September 18, 1953. She is the daughter of Richard and Pat (Goodreau) Radish. Kris received her bachelor's degree in journalism from the University of Wisconsin–Milwaukee, in 1975. She has worked as an educator and a journalist. She was a Pulitzer Prize finalist for Investigative Journalism. Her first book, *Run Bambi, Run: The Beautiful Ex-Cop and Convicted Murderer Who Escaped to Freedom and Won America's Heart*, was published in 1992.

Radish has two children, Andrew and Rachel Carpenter. She currently resides in Oconomowoc, Wisconsin.

Plot Summary: Attorney Katherine Givens is devastated to hear of the passing of her longtime friend Annie Freeman. When she receives a package containing Annie's red high-top sneakers containing her ashes, she is stunned. The package also contains a note asking her to contact four of Annie's other friends so that they might dispense of her ashes together. The five women travel from Sonoma, California, to New York City, sprinkling Annie's ashes at places of importance to her. Along the way, the women become good friends.

Publication Date: 2006

Number of Pages: 352

Geographic Setting: Sonoma, California, Florida, New Mexico, New York City.

Time Period: Present day

Series Notes: This is a stand-alone novel.

Subject Headings: Funeral rituals and ceremonies—Fiction; Inheritance and succession—Fiction; Female friendship—Fiction; Loss (psychology)—Fiction; Women travelers—Fiction; Bereavement—Fiction

Appeal Points: Overcoming grief, female friendship, self-discovery, and dark humor.

DISCUSSION QUESTIONS

- If you were going to send your friends on a journey to spread your ashes at the places that were most important in your life, where would they stop and why?
- Annie knew that funerals were for the living. What does she hope that each of the five women will gain from their journey?
- What do the women learn about Annie in Florida/New Mexico? New York City?
- Why do you suppose Annie kept the identity of the father of her children a secret? Why do you suppose she let his identity be discovered after his death?
- Each of the five women has something to overcome and learn. Discuss.

WEBSITE

http://www.krisradish.com

READERS' GUIDE

http://www.readinggroupguides.com/guides3/annie_freemans_funeral1.asp

READ-ALIKES

Berg, Elizabeth. *The Pull of the* Moon—for similar themes and tone.
Graham, Laurie. *The Future Homemakers of America*—for similar pacing and themes.
Julavits, Heidi. *The Effect of Living Backwards*—for dark humor, similar themes, and pacing.

Jeanne Ray

Step Ball Change

Jeanne Ray was born in 1940 in Nashville, Tennessee. She is a registered nurse at a clinic in Nashville. Writing is her second career. She is married and has two grown daughters, one of whom is the author Ann Patchett. Ray and her husband have 10 grandchildren.

Plot Summary: Sixty-something Caroline McSwain has the seemingly perfect life. She has a great husband and four grown children, in addition to owning her own dance studio. Things are about to get hectic for Caroline, however. Her sister Taffy's husband has left her for a younger woman, and her daughter Kay is marrying an extremely wealthy bachelor. On top of everything else, her house's foundation has cracked and she can't seem to get rid of her contractor.

Publication Date: 2002

Number of Pages: 240

Geographic Setting: Raleigh, North Carolina, and Atlanta, Georgia

Time Period: Present day

Series Notes: This is a stand-alone novel.

Subject Headings: Married people—Fiction; Triangles (interpersonal relations)—Fiction; Rich people—Fiction

Appeal Points: Light tone, humor, character-driven story, with witty dialogue.

DISCUSSION QUESTIONS

- The film rights to *Step Ball Change* have recently been purchased. If you were casting the film, who would you cast in what role and why?
- The foundation of the McSwain home is cracking. Describe how the foundation is used as a metaphor throughout the novel.

- Tom and Caroline eloped at the age of 20. This is in deep contrast with the wedding Kay is planning. Do you think Tom and Caroline's story has any impact on Kay's decision to have a huge wedding?
- What do you believe determines whether or not love will last?
- Two interracial couples are presented in the novel without any of the stereotypical complications one might expect in a novel about the South. Did this seem realistic to you?
- Who was your favorite secondary character and why?

WEBSITE

http://authors.simonandschuster.com/Jeanne-Ray/3026051

READERS' GUIDE

None available.

READ-ALIKES

Andrews, Mary Kay. *Savannah Blues*—for similar tone and character-driven storyline.
Arnold, Judith. *Love in Bloom*—for similar themes and tone.
Mapson, Jo-Ann. *Loving Chloe*—for similar themes and pacing.

Luanne Rice

The Deep Blue Sea for Beginners

Luanne Rice was born on September 25, 1955, in New Britain, Connecticut. She is the oldest of three daughters. She studied art history at Connecticut College. She has worked as a maid and a researcher. Her first novel, *Angels All Over Town*, was published in 1985. Five of Rice's novels have been adapted for television. She now splits her time between New York City and Old Lyme, Connecticut.

Plot Summary: Years ago, Lyra Davis left her wealthy life and all the expectations that came with it behind in order to live a more carefree lifestyle. She also left behind two young daughters in the care of her mother. Now in her teens, Pell has traveled to the Isle of Capri to confront the mother who abandoned her and demand some answers.

Publication Date: 2009

Number of Pages: 400

Geographic Setting: Capri, Italy

Time Period: Present day

Series Notes: This is a stand-alone novel.

Subject Headings: Mothers and daughters—Fiction; Abandonment (psychology)—Fiction; Reunions—Fiction; Family secrets—Fiction

Appeal Points: Strong female characters, homecomings, family dynamics, and a character-driven storyline.

DISCUSSION QUESTIONS

- Why did Lyra leave everything, including her daughters, behind? Do you believe a woman can ever justify leaving her children? Do you believe that Lyra was justified?

- Discuss the life that Pell and Lucy had under their grandmother's care. In what ways do you believe their life would have been different had Lyra stayed? What if she had taken the girls with her?
- In what ways does Max Gardner encourage Pell?
- Discuss Pell's relationship with Rafe.
- Discuss Lyra's relationship with her mother. In what ways does it differ from her relationship with her own daughters?

WEBSITE

http://luannerice.net/

READERS' GUIDE

None available.

READ-ALIKES

Berg, Elizabeth. *What We Keep*—for character-driven storyline and similar tone.

Bradford, Barbara Taylor. *Three Weeks in Paris*—for character-driven storyline and bittersweet tone.

McDermott, Alice. *At Weddings and Wakes*—for character-driven storyline and similar tone.

Lani Diane Rich

Wish You Were Here

Lani Diane Rich was born on June 7, 1971. She attended Syracuse University in New York. Before turning her hand to novel writing, she worked as a theater reviewer and freelance marketing consultant. Her first novel, *Time Off for Good* Behavior, was published in 2004. Rich lives in Syracuse, New York, with her husband and two daughters.

Plot Summary: Freya Daly's father sends to her Idaho to purchase a dilapidated campground. She needs to get this purchase off without a hitch if she hopes to win her father's approval and be able to take over his Boston-based real estate company. Unfortunately, Freya has run into trouble in the person of Nate Brody, the five-star chef who runs the campground. Nate made a promise to his dying father that he would never sell.

Publication Date: 2008

Number of Pages: 288

Geographic Setting: Idaho

Time Period: Present day

Series Notes: This is a stand-alone novel.

Subject Headings: Businesswomen—Fiction; Single women—Fiction; Idaho—Fiction

Appeal Points: Breezy tone, humor, believable characters, and a rich setting.

DISCUSSION QUESTIONS

- What is the cause of Freya's "condition?"
- Both Freya and Nate seem to want their fathers' approval. Why?
- Discuss Freya's relationship with Nate's daughter.
- The novel contains elements of both romance and mystery. Which element appealed more to you as a reader? Why?

- What is Uncle Malcolm's agenda?
- How has corporate life affected Freya? Does her reaction to the stress in her life ring true?

WEBSITE

http://www.lanidianerich.com

READERS' GUIDE

None available.

READ-ALIKES

Crusie, Jennifer. *Bet Me*—for similar tone and style.
Evanovich, Janet. *Love Overboard*—for similar tone and style.
Phillips, Susan Elizabeth. *Natural Born Charmer*—for similar tone and style.

Sherri Rifkin

LoveHampton

Before becoming a full-time writer, Rifkin worked as a cable television marketing executive at Bravo and Oxygen. She was also in charge of online marketing for HarperCollins and worked as an editor at both Harmony Books and Ballantine Books. Her credits include web and mobile content for a variety of television networks. She has also published two nonfiction books. She currently resides in New York City.

Plot Summary: Tori Miller is suffering from depression after losing her New York media job and being dumped by her boyfriend. She starts her own company but still cannot climb out of the sense of dread that has overcome her. Her three friends are putting together a pilot for a reality television show and decide to use Tori as their subject. She begins sharing a posh house in the Hamptons with five other 30-somethings. Hilarity and romance ensue.

Publication Date: 2008

Number of Pages: 312

Geographic Setting: Hamptons, New York

Time Period: Present day

Series Notes: This is a stand-alone novel.

Subject Headings: Women television producers and directors—Fiction; Roommates—Fiction; Summer resorts—Fiction; Hamptons (New York)—Fiction

Appeal Points: Fast pace, character-driven storyline, romance.

DISCUSSION QUESTIONS

- Tori wallows in self-pity for two years following her breakup with her boyfriend. Does this seem like a lot of time to you? What could she have done to overcome her depression sooner?

- In what ways does Tori jeopardize her friendships with Jerry, Jimmy, and Alice?
- In what ways was the novel similar to the television show *Sex in the City*?
- Discuss all of the characters in the house and their relationships to each other. What role does each of them play in the house?
- Who was your favorite character and why?
- Why do you think Tori originally chooses George? Does he have any redeeming qualities?
- Would you ever consider being on a reality television show? Why or why not?

WEBSITE

http://sherririfkin.com/

READERS' GUIDE

None available.

READ-ALIKES

Keyes, Marian. *The Other Side of the Story*—for similar themes and tone.
Moriarty, Liane. *The Last Anniversary*—for similar themes and style.
Rendahl, Eileen. *Balancing in High Heels*—for similar themes.

Nora Roberts

Red Lily

Nora Roberts was born on October 10, 1950, in Silver Spring, Maryland. Before turning her hand to writing, she worked as a secretary. Roberts has been named Best Contemporary Author by *Romantic Times*. She is the recipient of many awards, including the Gold Medallion and the RITA from Romance Writers of America. In 1986, she became the first author inducted into the Romance Writers of America Hall of Fame.

Roberts also writes a futuristic romantic suspense series under the name J. D. Robb. She currently lives in Keedysville, Maryland.

Plot Summary: Pregnant Haley moves to Memphis and takes a job at In the Garden Nursery. Her boss Roz and her coworker Stella help her re-establish herself and become good friends. Haley is happy with her new life and does not want to risk ruining it by acting on her attraction to Roz's son Harper. When she finally does, she is amazed to find out that not only is Harper also interested in her, but everyone in his family seems to be thrilled about their budding romance. Unfortunately, the ghost that resides at Harper House does not and seems determined to interfere with the couple's happiness.

Publication Date: 2005

Number of Pages: 371

Geographic Setting: Memphis, Tennessee

Time Period: Present day

Series Notes: In the Garden Trilogy, Book 3.

Subject Headings: Historic homes—Fiction; Haunted houses—Fiction; Ghosts—Fiction; Widows—Fiction; Gardening—Fiction; Female friendship—Fiction; Family relationships—Fiction

Appeal Points: Strong female characters in crisis, sexual tension, suspense, and fast-paced plot.

DISCUSSION QUESTIONS

- What is Haley running from when she moves to Memphis?
- Are there any similarities between Haley and Amelia?
- Why is Amelia so opposed to any of the Harper family members finding love?
- Discuss the progression of Harper's relationship with Amelia. How has it changed over the years?
- Discuss how the relationship between Haley and Amelia changes over the course of the novel.
- Have you read the previous two books in the trilogy? How do the other characters change in this story? Do you feel like having read the first two books helped your understanding of this story? If you haven't read the first two novels, will you go back and read them now?

WEBSITE

http://www.noraroberts.com

READERS' GUIDE

None available.

READ-ALIKES

Deveraux, Jude. *Someone to Love*—for similar themes.
Dominique, Ronlyn. *The Mercy of Thin Air*—for similar themes and tone.
Martin, Kat. *Scent of Roses*—for similar themes and tone.

Elisabeth Robinson

The True and Outstanding Adventures of the Hunt Sisters

Elisabeth Robinson is the independent producer and screenwriter of such films as *Braveheart* and *Last Orders*. She was born in Royal Oak, Michigan, and graduated from Oberlin College. *The True and Outstanding Adventures of the Hunt Sisters* is her first novel. Robinson currently lives in New York City.

Plot Summary: Olivia Hunt is trying to make it as a producer in Hollywood when she learns that her younger sister has been diagnosed with leukemia. Determined to be there for her sister, she flies back and forth from California to Ohio.

Publication Date: 2004

Number of Pages: 327

Geographic Setting: Hollywood, California, and Ohio

Time Period: Present day

Series Notes: This is a stand-alone novel.

Subject Headings: Women motion picture producers and directors—Fiction; Motion picture industry—Fiction; Married women—Fiction; Sisters—Fiction

Appeal Points: Biography, humor, plot, and character-driven storyline.

DISCUSSION QUESTIONS

- Why do you suppose that Robinson chose to write her novel in the form of letters? What do we learn about Olivia through her letters to the different people in her life?
- Robinson has been quoted as saying that the novel is based on her real-life relationship with her sister. Why do you suppose she chose to write it as fiction instead of a memoir?

- How does Olivia's image of her parents' marriage change when she goes back to Ohio?
- How are Olivia and Maddie different? How are they same?
- What legacy does Maddie leave behind?
- What do you think happens to Olivia and Maddie?

WEBSITE

This author does not have a website.

READERS' GUIDE

http://www.readinggroupguides.com/guides3/true_outstanding_hunt_sisters1.asp

READ-ALIKES

Berg, Elizabeth. *What We Keep*—for similar themes.
Brown, Rita Mae. *The Sand Castle*—for similar tone.
Crusie, Jennifer. *Welcome to Temptation*—for similar setting and tone

Barbara Samuel

The Goddesses of Kitchen Avenue

Barbara Samuel was born in 1959 in Colorado. She graduated from the University of Southern Colorado in 1985. She and her husband have two children. She published her first novel, *Strangers on a Train*, in 1989. The first book she wrote under her own name was *A Bed of Spices* in 1993.

Barbara Samuel has been the recipient of many awards and honors. She is a three-time RITA Award winner. She won the Janet Daily Award in 1996 for *The Last Chance Ranch*. In 1990, *Romantic Times* named her Romance Writer of the Year.

Plot Summary: Trudy, Jade, Roberta, and Shannelle have all suffered losses. Trudy has separated from her husband of 20 years. Jade has divorced her cheating husband. Roberta's husband has died, and Shannelle is unhappily married. These four residents of Kitchen Avenue form strong friendships and help each other on their individual journeys to self-discovery.

Publication Date: 2004

Number of Pages: 336

Geographic Setting: Colorado

Time Period: Present day

Series Notes: This is a stand-alone novel.

Subject Headings: Women—Colorado—Fiction; Man–woman relationships—Fiction; Female friendship—Fiction; Separated people—Fiction; Women boxers—Fiction

Appeal Points: Character-driven storyline, bittersweet and homespun tone, with lyrical writing.

DISCUSSION QUESTIONS

- Describe Trudy's relationship with Rick over the course of the novel.
- How is Trudy's fling with Angel any different from Rick's relationship with a younger woman?

- Why does Shannelle stay in her marriage when she is so unhappy?
- Why would Jade consider taking her cheating husband back?
- Which character in the novel do you most identify with, and why?
- How is each of the women in the novel empowered by the end of the story?

WEBSITE

http://www.barbarasamuel.com

READERS' GUIDE

None available.

READ-ALIKES

Berg, Elizabeth. *The Pull of the Moon*—for similar themes and characters.
Bohjalian, Chris. *The Buffalo Soldier*—for similar writing style and character-driven storyline.
Monroe, Mary Alice. *The Four Seasons*—for similar themes.

Lisa See

Snow Flower and the Secret Fan

Lisa See was born in Paris but grew up in Los Angeles. Her first book, *On Gold Mountain: The One Hundred Year Odyssey of My Chinese-American Family*, was published in 1995 and became a *New York Times* Notable Book. Her first novel, *Flower Net*, was published in 1997. She was named National Woman of the Year in 2001 by the Organization of Chinese American Women. She was also the recipient of the Chinese American Museum's History Makers Award in fall 2003.

In addition to her writing, See served as a guest curator for an exhibit on the Chinese-American experience for the Autry Museum of Western Heritage. She helped develop and curate the Family Discovery Gallery at the same museum. The gallery provides an interactive space for children and is based on Lisa's biracial, bicultural family. She has also designed a walking tour of Los Angeles Chinatown and written a companion guidebook. See currently resides in Los Angeles.

Plot Summary: Though they came from very different backgrounds, Lily and Snow Flower have always been very close friends. Over the years, they communicate in nu shu, a secret language known only to women. Their friendship is tested when the two girls marry and a secret is discovered.

Publication Date: 2005

Number of Pages: 258

Geographic Setting: China

Time Period: Nineteenth century

Series Notes: This is a stand-alone novel.

Subject Headings: Female friendship—Fiction; Women—China—Fiction; Married women—Fiction; Older women—Fiction; Footbinding—Fiction; Childbirth—Fiction; Secrecy—Fiction; Childbirth—Fiction

Appeal Points: Lyrical writing and attention to detail.

DISCUSSION QUESTIONS

- When they are very small, Madam Wang calls Lily and Snow Flower "old sames." Do you have an "old same?"
- Both Lily and Snow Flower are given arranged marriages. Discuss the ways in which their marriages differ.
- In nineteenth-century China, women's status was inferior to men's in both their birth families and their married families. Discuss examples of this as presented in the novel.
- Footbinding is done in order to make women more beautiful to men. In what ways do we make ourselves more appealing to men today? Compare and contrast.
- Lily and Snow Flower communicate using nu shu. Did you and your friends ever use a secret language of your own? What is the purpose of a secret language?

WEBSITE

http://www.lisasee.com/

READERS' GUIDE

http://www.readinggroupguides.com/guides3/snow_flower1.asp

READ-ALIKES

Chang, Lang Samantha. *Inheritance*—for similar themes.
McCunn, Ruthann Lum. *The Moon Pearl*—for similar themes.
Min, Anchee. *Empress Orchid*—for similar themes, subject matter, and writing style.

Christina Schwarz

Drowning Ruth

Christina Schwartz was born in Wisconsin. She received her bachelor's and master's degrees at Yale University in Connecticut. Following graduation, she taught in private schools in both Washington, D.C., and Los Angeles. She married Benjamin Schwartz in 1986. She and her husband now live in Boston, Massachusetts. Schwartz is known for her descriptions of setting and her slowly unfolding plotlines.

Plot Summary: Amanda and Mattie have chosen different paths. Married Mattie lives on a farm, raising her daughter on her own while her husband is away at war. Amanda went off to Milwaukee to work as a nurse tending wounded soldiers. Then Amanda returns home to the farm and forms a fierce bond with Mattie's daughter Ruth. Tragedy strikes when Mattie drowns in the lake and Amanda is left to raise her daughter.

Publication Date: 2000

Number of Pages: 338

Geographic Setting: Wisconsin

Time Period: 1919

Series Notes: This is a stand-alone novel.

Subject Headings: Drowning victims—Fiction; Mothers and daughters—Fiction; Farm life—Fiction; Sisters—Fiction; Wisconsin—Fiction

Appeal Points: Dark atmosphere and suspense.

DISCUSSION QUESTIONS

- The novel uses multiple points of view. What does this achieve? Did you find it confusing at all?
- Discuss how Carl's memory of Mattie changes over time.

- In what way does Schwarz build the suspense over the course of the novel?
- Discuss Ruth's relationship with her mother. What about her relationship with Amanda?
- Movie rights to the novel have been optioned. If you were in charge, who would you cast in which role?
- In what ways are the members of the community changed by Mattie's drowning?
- Discuss Ruth's memories of the night her mother drowned.

WEBSITE

This author does not have a website.

READERS' GUIDE

http://www.readinggroupguides.com/guides_D/drowning_ruth1.asp

READ-ALIKES

Berg, Elizabeth. *The Art of Mending*—for similar themes.
Berne, Suzanne. *The Ghost at the Table*—for similar themes.
Rendell, Ruth. *The Water's Lovely*—for similar themes.

Susan Sellers

Vanessa and Virginia

British-born author Susan Sellers is the product of a nomadic childhood, eventually running away to Paris. Sellers began writing as a child, writing in code so that her family couldn't read it. She has worked as a barmaid, tour guide, nanny, software translator, and cowriter on a film script with a Hollywood screenwriter. Sellers has a Ph.D. from the University of London and a D.E.A. from the University of Paris (Sorbonne). In 2002, she won the Canongate Prize for New Writing.

Sellers currently lives near Cambridge with her composer husband and young son. She is also a part-time professor in English literature at St. Andrews University.

Plot Summary: Sisters Vanessa Bell and Virginia Woolf grew in the shadow of their domineering father and the shoal moors of Victorian England. Upon their father's death, the two strike out on their own. Vanessa becomes a painter and Virginia becomes a writer. The two spend their entire lives in fierce competition, vying for the attention of their parents and brother and the members of the Bloomsbury group.

Publication Date: 2009

Number of Pages: 213

Geographic Setting: London, England

Time Period: Victorian England

Series Notes: This is a stand-alone novel.

Subject Headings: Sisters—Fiction; Women artists—Fiction; Women authors—Fiction; Bloomsbury group—Fiction; London (England)—Fiction

Appeal Points: Biographical novel, character-driven storyline, even pace, and emotional atmosphere.

DISCUSSION QUESTIONS

- After being sexually molested by her brother, Virginia enters into a sexless marriage with Leonard Woolf. He becomes a safe harbor for Virginia. What does Leonard gain from this marriage?
- The relationships among the members of the Bloomsbury Circle were extremely complicated. Discuss these.
- The relationship between Vanessa and Virginia is told through the eyes of Vanessa. How do you think the story might be different had it been told by Virginia? Why do you think Sellers chose to have the lesser known of the two sisters narrate the story?
- Why do you think Sellers chose to write this as a novel instead of a biography?
- Vanessa and Clive have an open marriage. What are your thoughts on open marriage versus monogamy?
- Virginia is quoted as saying, "A woman must have money and a room of one's own if she is to write fiction." Discuss in the context of the time period. How does it contrast with the needs of women today?
- Virginia was diagnosed as bipolar but never received treatment. How might her life have been different had she lived today?

WEBSITE

http://susansellers.wordpress.com/

READERS' GUIDE

None available.

READ-ALIKES

Giardina, Denise. *Emily's Ghost: A Novel of the Bronte Sisters*—for similar themes and tone.
Gregory, Philippa. *The White Queen*—for similar tone and pacing.
Vreeland, Susan. *The Forest Lover*—for similar themes and tone.

Linda Evans Shepherd and Eva Marie Everson

The Secret's in the Sauce

Linda Evans Shepherd is an American writer, international speaker, radio, and television host. She is the leader of the Advanced Writers and Speakers Association and Right to the Heart. Shepherd is the cofounder of Jubilant Press and publisher of *Right to the Heart of Women* e-zine. She has authored and coauthored 30 books.

Shepherd is from Denver, Colorado, and is married to her long-time husband Paul. They have two children.

Plot Summary: Friends Evangeline, Donna, Lisa, Lizzie, Goldie, and Vonnie start their own catering business. Secrets from each of the women's pasts come to the forefront as they try to hide them from each other. The situation threatens to tear apart not only their friendship but their business venture as well.

Publication Date: 2008

Number of Pages: 335

Geographic Setting: Summit View, Colorado

Time Period: Present day

Series Notes: Pot Luck Catering Club, Book 1

Subject Headings: Women's societies and clubs—Fiction; Caterers and catering—Fiction: Women cooks—Fiction; Cooking—Fiction; Female friendship—Fiction; Colorado—Fiction

Appeal Points: Character-driven and humorous tone.

DISCUSSION QUESTIONS

- Each of the women has a secret. What is it? Why does each of them feel as if she can't share it with the others?

- Discuss how Donna is treated by her half-brother and her boyfriend's mother.
- What was your favorite recipe in the book?
- Discuss how Summit View is a character in the novel.
- The novel is considered Christian fiction. How does Christianity manifest itself throughout the novel?

WEBSITE

http://www.shepro.com

READERS' GUIDE

http://www.readinggroupguides.com/guides_s/secrets_in_the_sauce2.asp

READ-ALIKES

Dessen, Sarah. *The Truth about Forever*—for similar themes.

Jackson, Neta. *The Yada Yada Prayer Group*—for similar themes and tone.

Smith, Virginia. *Third Time's a Charm*—for similar themes and tone.

Anita Shreve

Body Surfing

Anita Shreve was born in Dedham, Massachusetts, in 1946. She is the daughter of an airline pilot and a homemaker and is the oldest of three sisters. A graduate of Tufts University, Shreve worked as a high school teacher before beginning her writing career. Once a writer and editor for a number of New York magazines, she turned to freelance publishing in the New York area. Her first novel, *Eden Close*, was published in 1989. In 1998, Shreve received the PEN/L Winship Award and the New England Book Award for fiction.

Shreve met her future husband at age 13 and has two children and three stepchildren. She currently resides in Longfellow, Massachusetts.

Plot Summary: At 29, Sydney has already been divorced once and widowed once. Unable to handle it all, she quits graduate school and takes a summer job as a tutor to an 18-year-old developmentally delayed girl in a quiet oceanfront town in New Hampshire. Mr. Edwards, the father, tries to make her feel welcome, as do his two older sons, who take her body surfing and seem interested in Sydney in more romantic ways. When Julie disappears, tension mounts. Sydney and Jeff strike out to find her.

Publication Date: 2007

Number of Pages: 295

Geographic Setting: New Hampshire

Time Period: Present day

Series Notes: This is a stand-alone novel.

Subject Headings: Divorced women—Fiction; Widows—Fiction; Tutors and tutoring—Fiction

Appeal Points: Character-driven and emotional tone with lyrical writing.

DISCUSSION QUESTIONS

- Were you surprised when Julie ran away? Did the fact that she had a lesbian lover come as a complete shock to you?

- Mrs. Edwards is anti-Semitic and Sydney is half Jewish. Does this explain the way Mrs. Edwards treats Sydney, or do you think there are other factors at play?
- Discuss Sydney's relationship with both brothers. Does it make sense to you that she ends up making love with Jeff?
- When Ben learns about Jeff and Sydney's relationship, he is outraged. Discuss his response.
- Are Mrs. Edwards's expectations for Julie too high? Do parents always expect more from us than we are capable of?
- Discuss the theme of betrayal in the novel.

WEBSITE

http://www.anitashreve.com

READERS' GUIDE

http://litlovers.com/reading-guides/13-fiction/135-body-surfing-shreve

READ-ALIKES

Atwood, Margaret. *The Blind Assassin*—for similar tone and writing style.

Carey, Peter. *The History of the Kelly Gang*—for similar tone and writing style.

Giordano, Paolo. *The Solitude of Prime Numbers*—for similar tone and writing style.

Curtis Sittenfeld

American Wife

Curtis Sittenfeld was born in Cincinnati, Ohio. She attended Seven Hills School, where her mother was an art teacher, until eighth grade. She attended high school at the Groton Boarding School in Groton, Massachusetts. She graduated from Stanford University in 1997 with a degree in creative writing. Following graduation, she moved to Charlotte, North Carolina, where she worked for the *Charlotte Observer*. She has worked for *Fast Company* Magazine, attended the Iowa Writer's Workshop, and was the writer in residence at St. Alban's School in Washington, D.C., from 2002 to 2003. She has also worked as an English teacher.

Plot Summary: This fictionalization of the life of Laura Bush introduces readers to Alice Lindgren, a 31-year-old librarian with a past. After graduating from college, she meets Charlie Blackwell, the son of the Republican ex-governor of Wisconsin. She marries him a short month after their meeting. Charlie's family is everything Alice's is not. They are a large, loud family with deep-rooted beliefs. Things go fairly well until Charlie suffers a mid-life crisis and begins drinking heavily and using cocaine. Unwilling to live such a life, Alice takes her daughter and moves to her mother's. The separation hits Charlie hard and he gives up drinking and embraces evangelical Christianity. The two put aside their differences for the sake of their marriage. Charlie's career is on the upswing and Alice finds herself, first, the first lady of Wisconsin and then the first lady of the United States. Long-hidden secrets are threatened with exposure, and Alice finally takes a stand and goes public not only with her own secret but also with her opposition to the war in the Middle East.

Publication Date: 2008

Number of Pages: 592

Geographic Setting: Wisconsin, Washington, D.C.

Time Period: 1990s

Series Notes: This is a stand-alone novel.

Subject Headings: Presidents—United States—Wives; Domestic fiction

Appeal Points: Compelling first-person narrator and the human face of politics.

DISCUSSION QUESTIONS

- On page 3, Alice asks if she has made terrible mistakes. Has she? What do you think her mistakes were?
- Have you ever made compromises for someone you loved that you later regretted?
- How do the choices we make shape our future?
- On page 4, Alice says she leads a life "in opposition to itself." What do you think she means by this?
- Discuss, as Alice does, the idea of fame and its effect on people.
- What do you think Slice's life would have been like had Andrew lived?

WEBSITE

http://www.curtissittenfeld.com/

READERS' GUIDE

http://www.readinggroupguides.com/guides_A/American_Wife1.asp

READ-ALIKES

Hambly, Barbara. *The Emancipator's Wife*—for first-person narrative and the human side of a political marriage.

Niffenegger, Audrey. *The Time Traveler's Wife*—for first-person narrative and the theme of overcoming obstacles during marriage.

O'Brien, Patricia. *The Candidate's Wife*—for similar themes.

Lee Smith

The Last Girls

Lee Smith was born on November 1, 1944, in Grundy, Virginia. She is the daughter of Earnest Lee, a businessman, and Virginia, a teacher. Smith attended the Sorbonne and the University of Paris. She received her bachelor's degree in 1967 from Hollins College. Her first novel, *The Last Day the Dogbushes Bloomed*, was published in 1968.

Smith married James E. Seay, a poet, in June of 1967. Though they later divorced, she has two children from that marriage, Josh and Page. Smith later married Hal Crowther, a journalist, in June of 1985. The couple resides in Chapel Hill, North Carolina.

Plot Summary: Four friends reunite after 35 years to recreate a trip they took down the Mississippi River to New Orleans. One of the original group members has recently passed away, and the four remaining members intend to spread their friend's ashes along the way.

Publication Date: 2002

Number of Pages: 400

Geographic Setting: Mississippi

Time Period: 1999

Series Notes: This is a stand-alone novel.

Subject Headings: Women college graduates—Fiction; Female friendships—Fiction; Class reunions—Fiction; River boats—Fiction; Mississippi River—Fiction; Southern states—Fiction

Appeal Points: Character-driven storyline, bittersweet and humorous tone.

DISCUSSION QUESTIONS

- How has each of the four women changed since they last saw each other?
- When the novel was first published, *Publisher's Weekly* described it as "*The Big Chill* meets *Huck Finn*." Would you agree?

- The novel is set in the South. How do you think it would be different had it been set in the North?
- Do you think the women will ever fully understand Baby? Why does she remain such an enigma?
- What trouble does each individual woman face?

WEBSITE

http://www.leesmith.com/

READERS' GUIDE

http://www.readinggroupguides.com/guides3/last_girls1.asp

READ-ALIKES

Berg, Elizabeth. *The Last Time I Saw You*—for similar subject matter and themes.

King, Cassandra. *The Same Sweet Girls*—for similar themes, tone, and writing style.

Stokes, Penelope J. *Delta Belles*—for similar themes and subject matter.

Virginia Smith

Age Before Beauty

Before turning her hand to writing, Virginia Smith worked as a corporate director. She is the author of humorous Christian fiction. Her first novel, *Just As I Am*, was published in 2006. She and her husband Ted live in both Kentucky and Utah.

Plot Summary: Wanting to stay home with her newborn, Allie Harrod becomes an independent beauty consultant. She figures that way, she'll be home for all those milestones she doesn't want to miss with her baby and still contribute to the household income. Unfortunately, life doesn't seem to be going the way she planned. Her bank account is not looking very healthy and her husband is spending an awful lot of time with an attractive coworker. Thankfully, her sister is there to help her.

Publication Date: 2009

Number of Pages: 320

Geographic Setting: Kentucky

Time Period: Present day

Series Notes: Sister to Sister, Book 2.

Subject Headings: Motherhood—Fiction; Sisters—Fiction; Kentucky—Fiction

Appeal Points: Character-driven storyline, fast pace, and humor.

DISCUSSION QUESTIONS

- Allie has never much liked her mother-in-law. When she shows up on Allie's doorstep wanting to stay for a while, how does Allie handle the situation? How would you handle a similar situation?
- Is Allie's mother-in-law a stereotype?

- Allie wants to be the perfect wife, mother, sister, and daughter-in-law. Is there folly in this desire?
- Discuss Eric's reaction to his mother's presence.
- Can you relate to Allie's feelings after the birth of her baby? Do you think it is truly possible for a woman to have both a career and children?
- Discuss faith as it applies to each character in the novel.

WEBSITE

http://www.virginiasmith.org/

READERS' GUIDE

http://www.readinggroupguides.com/guides_a/age_before_beauty2.asp

READ-ALIKES

Evans, Richard Paul. *Finding Noel*—for similar themes and subject.
Kingsbury, Karen. *Just Beyond the Clouds*—for similar themes and subject.
Wick, Lori. *The Visitor*—for similar themes and subject.

Elizabeth Strout

Amy and Isabelle

Elizabeth Strout was born in Portland, Maine, in 1956. She was raised in small towns in Maine and New Hampshire. She is a graduate of Bates College, followed by a year in Oxford, England, before studying at law school for a year. Strout graduated with honors in 1982 from the Syracuse University College of Law and the Syracuse School of Social Work, obtaining both a law degree and a Certificate of Gerontology. She won the Pulitzer Prize for fiction in 2009 for *Olive Kitteridge*.

Strout is currently on the faculty of the MFA program at Queens University in Charlotte, North Carolina. She lives in New York City with her husband and daughter.

Plot Summary: Amy, who has just turned 16, feels nothing but distain for her mother, Isabelle, who is aloof and timid. For her part, Amy is somewhat shy and reserved until a substitute teacher pushes her to come out of her shell. That interaction awakens a sexuality in Amy that leads to an ill-conceived relationship with the man. The affair is discovered, and that discovery leads to an even larger chasm between Amy and Isabelle, who resents Amy for embracing a sexuality that she herself was unable to acknowledge.

Publication Date: 1999

Number of Pages: 304

Geographic Setting: Shirley Falls

Time Period: 1960s

Series Notes: This is a stand-alone novel.

Subject Headings: Mothers and daughters—Fiction; Extramarital relations—Fiction; High school teachers—Fiction; Small-town life—Fiction; High school students—Fiction; Mill towns—Fiction

Appeal Points: Lyrical writing, even pace, with realistic characters.

DISCUSSION QUESTIONS

- Discuss Isabelle's decision to move to Shirley Falls.
- Why does Isabelle feel set apart from the other residents of Shirley Falls?
- Isabelle has kept Amy fairly sheltered and feels stressed by her daughter's growing independence. Have you had to watch a child grow? Discuss your feelings at her or his impending independence.
- Did you ever have a crush on a teacher as a teenager? How did your feelings about teacher–student relationships change as you got older? As you had children of your own?
- Is there rivalry between Amy and Isabelle? What is the source of that rivalry?
- Several citizens of Shirley Falls harbor secrets. Discuss them.

WEBSITE

http://elizabethstrout.com/

READERS' GUIDE

http://www.readinggroupguides.com/guides_A/amy_and_isabelle1.asp

READ-ALIKES

Berg, Elizabeth. *The Art of Mending*—for similar themes and writing style.

Shreve, Anita. *Fortune's Rocks*—for similar subject matter and writing style.

Tan, Amy. *The Bonesetter's Daughter*—for similar themes and writing style.

Adriana Trigiani

Lucia, Lucia

Adriana Trigiani was born in Roseto, Pennsylvania. Her family moved to Big Stone Gap, Virginia, when she was six years old. Trigiani graduated from St. Mary's College in Indiana in 1981. She has worked as a play and television writer, a documentary film maker, a comic, a cook, an office worker, and a house cleaner. She is part of the comedy troupe the Outcasts. Her first novel, *Big Stone Gap*, was published in 2000.

Trigiani is married to television lighting designer Tim Stephenson. They have two daughters. She currently resides in New York City.

Plot Summary: Lucia Sartori is the only daughter of a prosperous Italian grocer. Wanting more than the life that has been prescribed for her, she takes a job as a seamstress at B. Altman's. When she learns that her fiancé's father expects her to quit her job after she marries, she breaks the engagement. Then she meets con man Jon Talbor. Following that unfortunate relationship, she plans to travel to California and start a new life, but her plans are thwarted when her mother falls ill.

Publication Date: 2003

Number of Pages: 256

Geographic Setting: Greenwich Village, New York City

Time Period: 1950s

Series Notes: This is a stand-alone novel.

Subject Headings: Italian-American Families—Fiction; Italian-American women—Fiction; Department stores—Fiction; Greenwich Village (New York City)—Fiction

Appeal Points: Strong sense of place, vivid characters, family dynamics, and rich detail.

DISCUSSION QUESTIONS

- Lucia wants more than to be a wife and mother. Do you think she made a mistake in ending her engagement to Dante?

- What role does each of Lucia's brothers play in the family?
- How does Lucia's story influence and affect Kit?
- To what extent is Lucia bound by the traditions she was raised with?
- Discuss religion as it is presented in the novel.
- How does Lucia change and grow over the course of the novel?

WEBSITE

http://www.adrianatrigiani.com

READERS' GUIDE

http://www.readinggroupguides.com/guides3/lucia_lucia1.asp

READ-ALIKES

Frank, Dorothea Benton. *Full of Grace*—for similar themes and subject matter.
Landvik, Lorna. *Oh My Stars*—for similar characters and witty dialogue.
Willett, Marcia. *The Birdcage*—for similar themes and character-driven storyline.

Joanna Trollope

Friday Nights

Joanna Trollope was born in England on December 9, 1943. She is the daughter of Arthur George Cecil and Rosemary (Hodson) Trollope. Trollope received her M.F.A. from Oxford University in 1965. Before publishing her first novel, Trollope worked as a teacher and as a clerk in a children's clothing store. She won the History Novel of the Year title from the Romance Novelist Association in 1979 for her first novel, *Eliza Stanhope*, which was published in 1978.

Joanna Trollope has been married twice and now lives on her own in London.

Plot Summary: Retired Eleanor invites two neighbors into her home to meet each other. That invitation develops over time into a sort of Friday night club and expands to include six women. The women become friends and help each other through various trials and tribulations until one of them becomes involved with a man who disrupts their comfortable club.

Publication Date: 2008

Number of Pages: 336

Geographic Setting: England

Time Period: Present day

Series Notes: This is a stand-alone novel.

Subject Headings: Female friendship—Fiction

Appeal Points: Character-driven storyline and romance, with realistic dialogue.

DISCUSSION QUESTIONS

- Paula and Toby reject Eleanor's offer to babysit but accept her invitation to come visit and meet each other. Why do they accept that invitation?

- How does Paula's budding romance change the group's dynamics?
- How does each of the women overcome her past?
- Which of the female characters do you most identify with? Why?
- Paula wants to distance herself from Toby's father but needs to continue having dealings with him for the sake of her son. Does she handle that relationship well? How would you handle a similar situation?

WEBSITE

http://www.joannatrollope.com

READERS' GUIDE

http://www.readinggroupguides.com/guides_F/friday_nights1.asp

READ-ALIKES

Binchy, Maeve. *The Glass Lake*—for similar writing style.
Monroe, Alice. *The Book Club*—for similar themes and tone.
Rice, Luanne. *Beach Girls*—for similar themes, characters, and tone.

Wendy Wax

Single in Suburbia

Born in St. Petersburg, Florida, Wendy Wax spent much of her youth on St. Pete beach. She learned to read at the age of five before starting school at Sunshine Elementary. She attended the University of Georgia, is a huge *Gone with the Wind* fan, and has even spoken at the Margaret Mitchell House. After college, she did work in radio, television, and film. Wax lives in Atlanta with her husband and two sons.

Plot Summary: Amanda, Brooke, and Candace have one thing in common: failed relationships. Amanda's husband has run off with a much younger woman. When she files for divorce, she finds out that the jerk has left her penniless. Brooke McKenzie may be married, but the fact that she married a recently divorced man at the age of 28 makes her a pariah in the eyes of the other trophy wives. To top it off, her stepson hates her. Candace Sugarman has been thrice divorced. She has it all—including a mother who treats her like a child. Amanda enlists the help of these two women in starting her own house-cleaning service. Not wanting any of her neighbors to know who she is, Amanda disguises herself and wins access to the homes of the rich and beautiful—who, it turns out, are not so wonderful as they would like others to believe.

Publication Date: 2006

Number of Pages: 367

Geographic Setting: Atlanta, Georgia

Time Period: Present day

Series Notes: This is a stand-alone novel.

Subject Headings: Single women—Fiction; Divorced women—Fiction; Single mothers—Fiction; Mother and child—Fiction; Single fathers—Fiction; Extramarital relations—Fiction; Secrets—Fiction; Deception—Fiction; Domestic workers—Fiction

Appeal Points: Humor and character-driven storyline.

DISCUSSION QUESTIONS

- Neither Amanda, Brooke, nor Candace fits into Atlanta society. What has happened to each of them to cause their outcast status?
- How does being in disguise help Amanda gain confidence?
- What moral dilemma is each of the characters facing?
- Discuss Amanda's relationship with her children.
- When Amanda's husband leaves her, she has no idea how to take care of herself financially. How important is it for a woman to be involved with the household finances? What do women give up when they choose the life of housewife and mother?
- Did Brooke make a mistake in hiding her past from her husband?
- Describe Candace's relationship with her mother.

WEBSITE

http://www.authorwendywax.com/

READERS' GUIDE

None available.

READ-ALIKES

Bond, Stephanie. *Body Movers*—for similar setting and tone.
Green, Jane. *Mr. Maybe*—for similar tone.
Keyes, Marian. *Lucy Sullivan Is Getting Married*—for similar tone and writing style.

Jennifer Weiner

In Her Shoes

Jennifer Weiner was born Jennifer Agnes Weiner on March 28, 1979, in De Ridder, Louisiana. She graduated summa cum laude from Princeton University in 1991. She then attended the Poynter Institute for Media Studies. Before publishing her first novel, *Good in Bed*, in 2001, she worked as a newspaper reporter and freelance writer. Weiner currently lives in Philadelphia, Pennsylvania, with her husband and two children, Lucy and Jane.

   In Her Shoes was made into a feature film starring Cameron Diaz in 2005.

Plot Summary: Sisters Maggie and Rose have a love/hate relationship. Rose has always been the responsible one while Maggie flitted from man to man and job to job. A rift between the two sends Maggie off to Boca Raton to spend time with the grandmother neither one of them knew they had.

Publication Date: 2002

Number of Pages: 424

Geographic Setting: Boca Raton, Florida, and Philadelphia, Pennsylvania

Time Period: Present day

Series Notes: This is a stand-alone novel.

Subject Headings: Sisters—Fiction; Florida—Fiction

Appeal Points: Humorous tone and quirky characters.

DISCUSSION QUESTIONS

- Discuss the relationship between Maggie and Rose. Rose is the older and more responsible of the two. Do you think birth order has anything to do with that?
- In what way has everyone enabled Maggie to be irresponsible?

- Why does Maggie and Rose's father keep the existence of their grandmother a secret?
- How does Maggie grow over the course of the novel?
- How does Rose grow over the course of the novel?
- Discuss the girls' relationship with their stepmother.

WEBSITE

http://www.jenniferweiner.com

READERS' GUIDE

http://www.readinggroupguides.com/guides3/in_her_shoes2.asp

READ-ALIKES

Alvarez, Julia. *Yo!*—for similar themes.
Delinsky, Barbara. *While My Sister Sleeps*—for similar themes.
Hannah, Kristin. *True Colors*—for similar themes.

Lauren Weisberger

Chasing Harry Winston

Lauren Weisberger was born in 1977. She received her bachelor's degree from Cornell University in 1999. She has worked as a personal assistant and a staff writer. She currently resides in New York City. Her first novel, *The Devil Wears Prada*, was published in 2003 and made into a movie featuring Anne Hathaway and Meryl Streep.

Plot Summary: Leigh, Adriana, and Emily are unsatisfied with their lives. Adriana has a bevy of rich boyfriends and has decided to choose among them. Emmy decides to have sex with several men in hopes of finding "the one." Leigh, a book editor, isn't sure how to go about changing her lot in life.

Publication Date: 2008

Number of Pages: 288

Geographic Setting: Manhattan, New York

Time Period: Present day

Series Notes: This is a stand-alone novel.

Subject Headings: Young women—Fiction; Female friendship—Fiction; Manhattan (New York)—Fiction

Appeal Points: Character-driven plot and humor.

DISCUSSION QUESTIONS

- The novel has been described as a *Sex in the City*. If that's true, which character in the novel corresponds with which character from the series?
- Each of the characters is about to turn 30. In what way does this milestone age hit them? Was there an age at which you questioned where you were in life?
- Which of the women do you most relate to and why?
- What does each of the women learn by the end of the novel?

- Have you ever made a pact with your friends? What was it about? Did you see it through to the end?

WEBSITE

http://www.laurenweisberger.com/

READERS' GUIDE

http://chickenlitbookclub.wordpress.com/2008/11/12/discussion-3-final-wrap
-up-chasing-harry-winston/

READ-ALIKES

Bushnell, Candace. *Lipstick Jungle*—for similar subjects, themes, and tone.
Kinsella, Sophie. *Twenties Girl*—for similar themes and tone.
McLaughlin, Emma. *The Nanny Diaries*—for similar setting and tone.

Michael Lee West

Mad Girls in Love: A Novel

Michael Lee West was born in Lake Providence, Louisiana. She was raised in New Orleans and Cookeville, Tennessee. She also spent a lot of her childhood in southern Mississippi, where both her parents and grandparents were from. West has a B.S. in nursing from the nursing school at East Tennessee State University and worked in the medical field until 1984 when her first son was born. She did some writing in notebooks and journals while at soccer, football, baseball, and basketball practice and had some poems published in the mid 1980s. Her first novel, *She Flew the Coop*, was published in 1994.

West and her husband currently live on a farm in Lebanon, Tennessee.

Plot Summary: Bitsy Wentworth hits her husband with a slab of ribs, then takes her daughter and flees. As a result, she loses custody of her child. Over the next 20 years, she forges a career as an interior decorator.

Publication Date: 2005

Number of Pages: 528

Geographic Setting: Crystal Falls, Tennessee

Time Period: 1972–1980s

Series Notes: Sequel to *Crazy Ladies*.

Subject Headings: Female friendships—Fiction; Southern states—Fiction

Appeal Points: Character-driven storyline and humor.

DISCUSSION QUESTIONS

- In what ways do mothers and daughters bond in the novel?
- Are any of the men in the novel likeable? Who?
- Have you read *Crazy Ladies*? If so, how did the characters change from that book to this one?

- Discuss Dorothy's letters to the First Ladies. What purpose do they serve?
- The novel takes place in the South. Would any of the women be drawn differently had it taken place elsewhere?
- What role does forgiveness play in the novel?

WEBSITE

http://michaelleewest.com/content/index.asp

READERS' GUIDE

http://www.readinggroupguides.com/guides3/mad_girls_in_love1.asp

READ-ALIKES

Bradford, Barbara Taylor. *Unexpected Blessings*—for similar themes.
Frank, Dorothea Benton. *Return to Sullivan's Island*—for similar themes and style.
Reynolds, Sheri. *Firefly Cloak*—for similar themes.

Madeleine Wickham

The Wedding Girl

Madeleine Wickham was born Madeleine Townley in 1969. She graduated from Putney High School and earned a degree in P.P.E. from New College in Oxford, England, in 1990. Before turning to fiction, she worked as a financial journalist. At the age of 24 while still working as a journalist, she finished her first novel, *The Tennis Party*, which became a top-10 best seller. Most recently, she has written novels under the name Sophie Kinsella.

Wickham lives in Surrey and London with her husband of 17 years, Henry, a boys' prep school headmaster, and their four sons.

Plot Summary: Years ago, Milly spent a semester at Oxford and befriended two male students who were in love. She agreed to marry one of them so that he could stay in the country. Following the wedding, they disappeared from her life and she has barely given them a thought since then. Now she is about to marry her true love, but a bitter photographer with proof of her past is threatening to expose her secret.

Publication Date: 2009

Number of Pages: 32

Geographic Setting: England

Time Period: Present day

Series Notes: This is a stand-alone novel.

Subject Headings: Weddings—Planning—Fiction; Impediments to marriage—Fiction

Appeal Points: Humor, fast pace, and character-driven story.

DISCUSSION QUESTIONS

- How does each character view marriage?
- Discuss Milly and Isobel's relationship with their father.

- Discuss Simon's relationship with his father.
- Have you ever kept a secret that came back to bite you? What was it? Why did you keep it?
- Was Milly's expectation that her marriage to Allan could be kept secret realistic?
- Why do you think Isobel won't reveal the name of her baby's father?

WEBSITE

http://www.sophiekinsella.co.uk/

READERS' GUIDE

http://litlovers.com/reading-guides/13-fiction/1116-wedding-girl-wickham

READ-ALIKES

Carr, Robin. *The Wedding Party*—for similar subject and tone.
Lockwood, Cara. *I Do, But I Don't*—for similar subject and tone.
Webb, Sarah. *Always the Bridesmaid*—for similar tone.

Sherryl Woods

Stealing Home

Sherryl Woods was born on July 23, 1944, in Washington, D.C. She received her bachelor's degree in 1966 from Ohio State University. Before becoming a novelist, she worked as a newspaper representative and a television and radio editor. She currently resides in Key Biscayne, Florida.

Woods is an prolific ovelist. In addition to writing under her own name, she has also written under the names Alexandra Kirk and Suzanne Sherril. Her first novel under her own name, *Jamaican Midnight*, was published in 1984.

Plot Summary: Maddie Townsend's doctor husband got his nurse pregnant. Following their divorce, she has a difficult time finding a job. Her friends offer to finance a gym for women if Maddie will manage it. Things seem to be getting better until her oldest son Ty starts having trouble in school and his coach calls her in for a conference. The two begin a relationship but have to deal with tongues wagging in their small town.

Publication Date: 2007

Number of Pages: 400

Geographic Setting: South Carolina

Time Period: Present day

Series Notes: Sweet Magnolia series, Book 1.

Subject Headings: Single mothers—Fiction; Divorced women—Fiction; Man–woman relationships—Fiction; South Carolina—Fiction

Appeal Points: Relaxed pace, heartwarming story with a strong sense of place.

DISCUSSION QUESTIONS

- Why do the townsfolk disapprove of Maddie's relationship with Cal?
- How does the divorce affect Ty? How does it affect Maddie?

- Does the age difference between Maddie and Cal matter? Would the townsfolk have the same reaction if Cal were the older of the two?
- Why does Maddie's husband question the choice he has made?
- Have you ever been divorced or do you know someone who is divorced? Were the feelings and experiences presented in the novel authentic to you?
- Do you think the characters in town were believable? Would they have been as believable had the novel taken place in a city?

WEBSITE

http://www.sherrylwoods.com/

READERS' GUIDE

None available.

READ-ALIKES

Bretton, Barbara. *Someone Like You*—for similar subject and tone.
Crusie, Jennifer. *Tell Me Lies*—for similar subject and themes.
Macomber, Debbie. *74 Seaside Avenue*—for similar setting and tone.

Cathy Yardley

L. A. Woman

Cathy Yardley was an art history and mass communications major at University of California, Berkley, where she received her bachelor's degree. Before writing novels, she worked as an advertising assistant, a project manager, a marketing manager, and a budget analyst. Her first novel, *The Cinderella Solution*, was published in 2000. Yardley currently resides in San Leandro, California.

Plot Summary: Twenty-five-year-old Sarah Walker's fiancé Benjamin convinces her to leave northern California and move to L.A. There, she gets an entry-level job and waits for him to join her. It turns out that Benjamin hasn't actually convinced his boss to let him relocate yet. Sarah can't make ends meet on her own, so she decides to share an apartment with a woman named Martika. Martika is a party girl, polar opposite of the quiet Sarah, and though the two get along well enough, they're not exactly friends. When Sarah decides she's had enough of waiting for Benjamin, she dumps him and is tutored by Martika in the fine art of being an "L.A. woman."

Publication Date: 2002

Number of Pages: 258

Geographic Setting: Los Angeles, California

Time Period: Present day

Series Notes: This is a stand-alone novel.

Subject Headings: Young women—Fiction; Single women—Fiction; Temporary workers—Fiction; Nightclubs—Fiction

Appeal Points: Quick read, spunky writing, humorous dialogue.

DISCUSSION QUESTIONS

- At Benjamin's prompting, Sarah quits her job and moves from northern California to LA. Would you ever up and move your life for a man?

- Discuss Sarah's relationship with Benjamin.
- Sarah and Martika are polar opposites. Describe the ways that they are different. In what ways are they similar?
- Describe Sarah's relationship with her best friend, Judith.
- The chapters in the novel are named for Doors songs. Why do you think the author did that? Does it work?
- Describe Sarah's relationship with her friend Taylor.
- Yardley tells the tale using the third-person narrative. Did that work for you? Would you have preferred it had it been written in the first person?
- What would you, or wouldn't you do for love?

See standard questions in the Introduction for more questions.

WEBSITE

http://cathyyardley.com/

READERS' GUIDE

None available.

READ-ALIKES

Bushnell, Candace. *Lipstick Jungle*—for similar tone and style.
Kinsella, Sophie. *The Undomestic Goddess*—for similar tone and style.
Street, Libby. *Happiness Sold Separately*—for similar tone and style.

Chapter 2
**24 Additional Women's Fiction,
Chick Lit, and Romance Titles
to Consider for Discussion**

Catherine Anderson, *Summer Breeze* (2006)

Five years ago, Rachel's entire family was slaughtered and she received a bullet wound to the head. The killer has never been identified. Since that time, she has not left her home. When her farmhand is shot, her neighbor vows to keep Rachel safe. When he does not get a response after knocking on Rachel's door, he enters through her bedroom window and does not receive the most welcoming of hellos. Despite Rachel's fear and hard exterior, Joseph has the feeling that she is a woman he will have a hard time getting over.

Margaret Atwood, *The Handmaid's Tale* (1986)

In the near future, the United States is now called the Republic of Gilead. The role of women is now decided by their ability to produce offspring. Offred, once a woman with a job, a husband, and a child of her own, is now a handmaid. She lives with the Commander and his wife and must submit to a ceremony once a month in which she prays that she becomes pregnant.

Anjali Banerjee, *Invisible Lives* (2006)

Indian-American Lakshmi Sen has the ability to sense what other people are longing for. This ability comes in handy in her work making saris at Mystic Elegance, her mother's shop. Wishing to please her mother and honor her deceased father, she agrees to an arranged marriage with an Indian doctor. Then a famous client comes into the store and Lakshmi falls in love with the actress's very American chauffer.

Melissa Bank, *The Wonder Spot* (2005)

Sophie Applebaum is the black sheep of the family. In a series of vignettes, readers follow Sophie through her varying roles as middle child and best friend to the popular girl, her immersion in New York City, and her father's death. The stories span 25 years of Sophie's coming-of-age story.

Chris Bohjalian, *Midwives* (1997)

Sybil Danforth had successfully delivered more than 500 babies. One cold March evening, a woman in labor is unable to make it to the hospital. By the time Sybil arrives, the woman has had a stroke and Sybil performs an emergency C-section to save the child. When her assistant tells the police that the mother was still alive when the operation was performed, Sybil finds herself on trial for murder. The novel is told through the eyes of Sybil's now grown daughter, an OB/GYN.

Pearl Cleage, *Babylon Sisters* (2005)

Catherine Sanderson has put together a successful and fulfilling life for herself and her daughter Phoebe. The only strain on their relationship is the fact that Catherine has refused to answer any of her daughter's questions about who her father might be. The man in question, B. J. Johnson, has been in Africa on assignment as a news reporter for all these years. Now he has come home to Atlanta to crack a story and has asked Catherine for her help. How can she reveal to him the feelings she still has and let him know about the daughter he never knew he had?

Annie Downey, *Hot and Bothered* (2006)

The life of a mother of two in her late 30s is thrown into turmoil when her sex-addict ex-husband continues to show up at her door. Throw in an alcoholic best friend and an offbeat mother, and you've got a recipe for disaster until she decides to take control over her own life.

Pai Kit Fai, *The Concubine's Daughter* (2009)

Li-Xia's dead mother was a concubine who wanted more for her daughter. Li-Xia escapes death and grows up in a rice shed. When she turns eight, she refuses to have her feet bound and is sold to a silk merchant, where she finds friendship with the other workers. A sea captain secures her freedom and allows her to travel on his ship. The two marry and she is able to fulfill her dream to learn to read and write.

Dorothea Benton Frank, *The Land of Mango Sunsets* (2007)

Miriam Swanson's life has been anything but rosy since her cheating husband divorced her. She has virtually no relationship with her two grown sons, and things at work are not much better. Her boss is her ex-best friend. To complicate matters, she catches the woman's husband in the arms of another woman. After retreating to the South Carolina island home of her youth, she finally reveals what she saw to her boss, with disastrous results.

Laurie Graff, *You Have to Kiss a Lot of Frogs* (2004)

This novel follows the adventures of actress Karrie Kline as she navigates the world of dating, her move from New York City to Los Angeles, her conversion to Judaism, and a bevy of hilarious suitors.

Laurie Graham, *The Future Homemakers of America* (2002)

Five very different women, all Air Force wives, meet during the 1940s and forge a friendship that lasts the next 50 years. The women see each other through the death of husbands, alcoholism, extra-marital affairs, and child rearing.

Elise Juska, *One for Sorrow, Two for Joy* (2007)

Crossword puzzle writer Claire Gallagher's marriage to a respected scientist has been polite and strained at best. She has always wanted to finish her dissertation but has lapsed into a semifulfilling life. Then one day, she announces that she is leaving the marriage. At the prompting of her sister, she travels to her ancestral home of Ireland.

Beth Kendrick, *Fashionably Late* (2006)

Twenty-five-year-old Becca Davis has always been interested in fashion but has never had the nerve to take the leap and do something with her talent. When her controlling boyfriend proposes, she says yes, then immediately regrets her decision. Breaking it off, she moves from Phoenix to Los Angeles, where she moves in with her sister Claire and tries to get her designing career off the ground.

Mia King, *Sweet Life* (2008)

All has not been going well in Marissa Price's world. She and her husband have been having some serious problems, and she and her daughter just don't seem to bond. When her husband gets a new job that relocates them to Hawaii, she feels it will be a second chance to make things right. Then they arrive and her husband tells her he thinks he needs some time away from her.

Cathy Lamb, *Such a Pretty Face* (2010)

At age 32, Stevie Barrett suffered a heart attack. Since then, she's undergone bariatric surgery and lost 170 lbs. With her new body comes a new life and new challenges as she and those around her struggle to figure out who she really is.

Carole Matthews, *With or Without You* (2004)

Baby magazine editor Lyssa Allan wants nothing more than a baby of her own. Her live-in boyfriend Jake is happy to comply until a round of IVF treatments fails and he declares that he's had enough. Lyssa moves in with her sister and six children, then takes off to climb the Himalayas in a hilarious journey of self-discovery.

Joyce Meyer, *Any Minute: A Novel* (2009)

Sarah Harper has tried to be it all, and her desire to be successful has kept her at arm's length from her husband and children. A terrible car accident leaves her presumed dead, but her spirit is just on the other side. While there, she learns things that transform her, and she is a different woman entirely when she is revived.

Sue Miller, *The Good Mother* (1986)

Anna Dunlap is the recently divorced mother of four-year-old Molly. When she meets Leo, she feels like a more than a mother for the first time. He awakens in her feelings long forgotten, and she revels in his attention and the new family that they forge together. When shocking events threaten to destroy that family, she and the reader must determine what it is that makes one a good mother.

Jane Moore, *The Second Wives Club* (2006)

Fiona, Alison, Julia, and Susan join together to form the Second Wives Club. Each of them is struggling in some way. They help each other through their husbands' friendships with their ex-wives, problems with stepchildren, and custody issues.

Erica Orloff, *Mafia Chic* (2004)

Teddi Gallo may have been born into a mafia family, but she's tried to keep her life on the straight path. She and her cousin run their own restaurant and have made sure to keep their "family" out of their business. Unfortunately, the FBI seems all too interested in the restaurant. Fortunately, agent Mark Petrocelli seems awfully interested in her. Now if she could only keep her family out of her personal business, she'd be all set.

Jane Porter, *She's Gone Country* (2010)

Shey Darcy's husband has left her—not for another woman, but for another man. Left bereft and feeling slightly less than her former ex-supermodel self, she packs up her three sons and moves home to Texas. There, she finds work as a catalog model and reunites with an old flame.

Monica Pradhan, *The Hindi-Bindi Club* (2007)

Three Indian-American women live very different lives than their parents. All have married American men. When one of them gets divorced, she considers that perhaps the old ways are not so wrong and asks her parents to arrange a marriage for her.

Liz Rosenberg, *Home Repair* (2009)

Eve's husband walks out on her in the middle of a garage sale, leaving her with his two young sons. Her mother comes to help, causing even more stress in Eve's life. Old and new friends help her navigate uncharted territories as she discovers that maybe, just maybe, she's found a better life after all.

LaVyrle Spencer, *Family Blessings* (1993)

When Chris Lallek's best friend and fellow police officer Greg Reston is killed in a car accident, Chris proves invaluable to his siblings and widowed mother. His relationship with Greg's mother Lee develops into a romantic one. When he proposes marriage, Lee must decide if their relationship is really based on love or mutual mourning.

Notes

ACKNOWLEDGMENTS

1. MLS Readers' Advisory Genre Study. Web. http://ragenrestudy.wordpress.com/.

INTRODUCTION

1. "Women's Fiction." *Wikipedia*. Web. http://en.wikipedia.org/wiki/Women%27s_fiction. 5/27/2011.

2. North, Anna. "Blogger Asks, What Is Women's Fiction?" *Jezebel*. Web. http://jezebel.com/5278713/blogger-asks-what-is-womens-fiction. 5/23/2011.

3. Camacho, Kristie. "What Is Women's Fiction?" *National*. Web. http://www.examiner.com/fiction-in-national/what-is-women-s-fiction. 5/21/2011.

4. "About the Romance Genre." *Romance Writers of America*. Web. http://www.rwa.org/cs/the_romance_genre. 5/3/2011.

5. *In the Classroom or In the Bedroom Chick Lit: The New Woman's Fiction.* Edited by Suzanne Ferriss and Mallory Young. Routledge Publishing, 2005. 288 pages. Trade Paperback. Reviewed by Jessica Lynice Hooten.

6. Vnuk, Rebecca. "Collection Development 'Chick Lit': Hip Lit for Hip Chicks." *Library Journal*. Web. http://www.libraryjournal.com/article/CA623004.html. 5/18/2011.

Appendix A
Sample Book Group Handout

Circle of Grace

Penelope J. Stokes

Circle of Grace is the story of four women friends who have lost touch since college. When one of them learns she is dying of cancer, she invites the others to North Carolina for a reunion. Over the course of the weekend, each woman reveals the truth about her life and earns acceptance from the others.

While You Read the Novel think about the following questions:

1. How has your life changed since you were in college? Has your life turned out differently than you expected it to?
2. If you were told you were dying of an incurable disease, whom would you want to visit with? Why? What would you want to discuss with those people?
3. What part does the setting play in the novel? Grace, Lovey, Liz, and Tish went to college in the South. How do you think their lives would have been different had it been set somewhere else?
4. The author divides the novel into four sections, each narrated by one of the four women. Do you consider all of the women reliable narrators? Why or why not?
5. Which one of the four women do you most relate with and why?
6. Would you read another book by this author?
7. Who do you know that you would recommend this book to?

Appendix B
List of Reader Resources

All About Romance—Book reviews, a list of new releases by month, a bulletin board, polls, an "If You Like" section, writing contests, and more.
http://www.likesbooks.com/

Bookspace—"If You Like This . . ." lists from the Hennepin County Library in Minnesota.
http://www.hclib.org/pub/bookspace/FindAGoodBook.cfm

Boone County Public Library—The Boone County Public Library offers read-alikes by author, genre, and title. You can also search for novels set in a particular state.
http://www.bcpl.org/advisory/books/read-alikes/

Overbooked—Reading recommendations, reviews, links, and special features.
http://www.overbooked.org/ra/index.html

Read This!—From the Peabody Institute Library in Danvers, Massachusetts. Current author information, book lists, and reviews.
http://danversreads.wordpress.com/

Readers' Corner—The Morton Grove Public Library's "webrary." Includes links to websites for book lovers, book reviews, book lists, book discussion guides, and more.
http://www.webrary.org/rs/rslinks.html

The Romance Reader—Reviews, reviews, and more reviews! Departmentalized by subgenre.
http://www.theromancereader.com/

Seattle Public Library—Read-alikes, reading lists, and Pearl's Picks from librarians at the Seattle Public Library.
http://www.spl.org/

Appendix C
List of Book Group Resources

Ballantine Readers' Circle—Author interviews and discussions for titles published by Ballantine.
  http://bantam-dell.atrandom.com/

Book Group Corner—Reading group guides from Random House's Bantam, Dell, Doubleday, and Broadway imprints.
  http://bantam-dell.atrandom.com/

Hachette Reading Group Guides—Offers discussion questions for books published by Hachette.
  http://www.hachettebookgroup.com/books_bookclubreadingguides.aspx

Macmillan—Plot summaries and discussion questions for titles published by Macmillan.
  http://us.macmillan.com/readinggroupgold.aspx

Mostly We Eat Book Club—Maintained by a group of friends who have met to discuss books and eat. The site contains information on how they choose their books and gives a list of what they have read and eaten over the years.
  http://mostlyweeat.org/

Random House—Reading guides for titles published by Vintage and Anchor Books.
  http://reading-group-center.knopfdoubleday.com/

Reading Group Choices—An excellent source of material for reading groups: how to start a book group, music suggestions to accompany books, plot summaries, author information, and discussion questions.
  http://www.readinggroupchoices.com/

Reading Group Gold—Reading group guides from Macmillan Publishers.
  http://us.macmillan.com/readinggroupgold.aspx

Reading Group Guides—Maintained by publishers and reading group consultants.
  http://www.readinggroupguides.com/content/index.asp

Simon & Schuster—Discussion questions for titles published by Simon & Schuster.
  http://readinggroups.simonandschuster.com/

W. W. Norton—Discussion questions for nonfiction and fiction published by Norton.
  http://books.wwnorton.com/books/reading-guides-list.aspx?tid=3288

Subject Index

Author Index

Title Index

Geographic Setting Index

About the Author

NANCI MILONE HILL is the Director of the Boxford Town Library in Boxford, Massachusetts. She co-edits the Perspectives column for *Public Libraries*, writes the Christian Fiction column for *Library Journal*, and is a regular contributor to *NoveList*.

CPSIA information can be obtained at www.ICGtesting.com
Printed in the USA
LVOW10s2154220114

370618LV00004B/31/P